A BEAUTIFUL ADVENTURE MARRIAGE

A BEAUTIFUL ADVENTURE MARRIAGE

A Guide for the Marriage God Created for You

Tara Lorai Payne
with Alex Payne

ELM HILL

A Division of
HarperCollins Christian Publishing

www.elmhillbooks.com

A Beautiful Adventure Marriage
A Guide for the Marriage God Created for You

Published in Nashville, Tennessee, by Elm Hill, an imprint of Thomas Nelson. Elm Hill and Thomas Nelson are registered trademarks of HarperCollins Christian Publishing, Inc.

Elm Hill titles may be purchased in bulk for educational, business, fund-raising, or sales promotional use. For information, please e-mail SpecialMarkets@ ThomasNelson.com.

Scripture quotations marked AMP are from the Amplified˚ Bible. Copyright © 1954, 1958, 1962, 1964, 1965, 1987 by The Lockman Foundation. Used by permission. (www.Lockman.org)

Scripture quotations marked ERV are taken from the Easy-to-Read Version. Copyright © 2006 by Bible League international.

Scripture quotations marked ESV are from the ESV˚ Bible (The Holy Bible, English Standard Version˚). Copyright © 2001 by Crossway, a publishing ministry of Good News Publishers. Used by permission. All rights reserved.

Scripture quotations marked NIV are from the Holy Bible, New International Version˚, NIV˚. Copyright © 1973, 1978, 1984, 2011 by Biblica, Inc.˚ Used by permission of Zondervan. All rights reserved worldwide. www.Zondervan.com. The "NIV" and "New International Version" are trademarks registered in the United States Patent and Trademark Office by Biblica, Inc.˚

Scripture quotations marked NLT are from the Holy Bible, New Living Translation. © 1996, 2004, 2007, 2013, 2015 by Tyndale House Foundation. Used by permission of Tyndale House Publishers, Inc., Carol Stream, Illinois 60188. All rights reserved.

Library of Congress Cataloging-in-Publication Data

Library of Congress Control Number: 2020900939

N 978-1-400330263 (Paperback)
˚78-1-400330270 (eBook)

For my Mama~ the first author I ever loved!
Thank you for leading the way!

Marriage is God's idea!
It's a good idea and it
can be a beautiful
adventure!

CONTENTS

THE ADVENTURE OF A LIFETIME

In 2009, I was presented with the adventure of a lifetime. My church was joining another church to go on a ten-day trip to Israel in the fall of 2010. A friend of mine had taken the same trip a few years prior and had shared her experience with me. From the moment I looked at the first picture, I had this burning desire inside of me. I knew I had to go. I had to experience this for myself. The trip cost about three thousand dollars. I signed up immediately, not knowing how I was going to pay for it.

At the time, I taught at a small Christian school. I was happy, but broke. My mother and I lived together on a fixed income. We started praying and my mother started writing people we knew asking for sponsorships. By the time January rolled around, I had saved about 350 dollars. It had taken a few months to save that small amount, most of it was Christmas money, but the trip was not until November. It gave me hope that this was a possibility. Little did I know the Lord was about to ask me to do one of the hardest things I've ever had to do.

Every January, my church does a First Fruits Fast. We fast and pray for 21 days, then we do a special offering for the new year. This is just our way of starting off a new year, by dedicating the first few weeks of it to the Lord. The Lord always shows up during this time.

I knew exactly what I was going to fast and pray about. We had a special New Year's Eve service that year. During the service, I ask the Lord what He wanted me to give for my First Fruits Offering. I always ask early because, usually, it takes some time before He tells me what to give. Well, not this year. He instantly answered me. He told me to give the 350 dollars I had saved for Israel.

I'll never forget that moment. I could take you to the exact seat I was sitting in when He told me. Everything is as clear to me now, as it was 9 years ago. I was speechless, as if every bit of air was sucked from the room. I didn't want to believe what I heard. Surely, I had misunderstood. So, I asked again and again, and I got the same answer. I would love to say my heart exploded at that moment with joyful obedience and agreement, but it didn't. Quite the opposite happened. A feeling of fear and desperation fell on me. I questioned and argued with Him about it. I asked Him if He realized this was the money I had saved for the trip. He knew. I asked Him if He realized how hard it was going to be for me to come up with all the money. He knew. I pointed out how much harder it was going to be if I gave this money away. He assured me; He knew all these things. However, His answer didn't change. I would like to tell you the questioning and arguing stopped right then, but for the next three weeks I walked around asking if He was completely sure about the offering He wanted me to give. He was sure. First Fruits Sunday came, and I was obedient. I gave all the money I had saved in the offering. I literally cried as I walked to the altar. By this time, I knew what I had to do, but it was still hard. As I laid the money down, I prayed a simple little prayer. "Lord, I am giving you everything. Please let Israel happen."

I started saving again, but something interesting happened. Tax season came and it did not bring good news with it. When we filed our taxes, it came back that we owed money and would not get a refund. I remember the "feels" of that moment clearly. Now we had taxes and Israel money to pay. I didn't have the money for either. I thought for sure Israel wouldn't happen. Despite my discouragement, the Lord was very clear with me. He was in control and I was not to speak anything negative over the situation. It was one of the hardest things to do, but I didn't say anything, to anyone about it. I was so afraid I would say something negative that I intentionally didn't talk about it at all. I bought a tiny notebook, wrote scriptures in it, and put it in my purse. Anytime fear or doubt showed up, I would get my notebook out and read a scripture. Then I would repeat "Lord, I trust You," out loud.

To this day, what happened next blows my mind. To be honest with you the math still does not add up. By March, everything was paid. In one month, the taxes and the entire Israel trip were completely paid for. The money came in from the sponsors my mother had written, and we received unexpected checks in the mail from overpaid bills. It made no sense at all, but it was amazing. A total miracle! It was God showing me that He really was in control. During that time, He showed me Ephesians 3:20-21 is true. If you give Him what little you have, He can go above and beyond what we could even ask for or imagine. Looking back at it now, I believe this whole miracle came from that first act of obedience. If I hadn't been obedient with the first 350 dollars, none of this would have happened.

I was going to Israel! I was so excited to see the Holy Land and go to the places I had read about so many times. Because of everything the Lord had done to make this trip possible, I knew it was going to be amazing. I had been blessed so BIG with just the opportunity to go. If the Lord had just stopped there it would've been great, but as it would turn out the Lord specializes in BIGGER. He was not done blessing me yet.

I was standing in the airport, waiting to board the plane, when I saw this handsome man in our group. I had seen him before, but this time he caught my attention. I remember thinking he was cute, but I instantly thought, "You are going to Israel, stop it!". So, I put it in the back of my mind and got on the plane. The next seven days were absolutely amazing. We went to the Sea of Galilee, Capernaum,

Jericho, Bethlehem, and Jerusalem. There is just something about being in Israel that is captivating. I have never been so far away from home yet so at home. It's a place everyone should experience!

On the 7th day, we went into Jerusalem. We went to the Western Wall to pray before we explored the rest of the city. My Pastor had told us to write down what we were believing God for on a piece of paper. After we prayed, we could leave the paper there at the wall. There were several things on my list, but one of them was for God to give me a godly husband. I had been praying for a husband for several years, but nothing seemed to be happening. I prayed, placed my piece of paper in the wall, and returned to the group ready to go to the next location. We left the Western Wall and went to the Pool of Bethesda where Jesus healed the lame man in John 5. We spent time there praying as a group and for individuals. I was standing over to the side when my pastor approached me with the handsome man from the airport. Pastor looked at me and said, "Alex is going through some of the same things you are. I think he needs to pray for you." With that statement, he joined our hands together and walked away. So, there we were, holding hands, staring at each other, not entirely sure what to do. Alex did what Pastor told him too. He prayed for me, we side hugged (because that's what Christians do after we pray for someone), and then he walked away. It was a seemingly simple interaction.

After we left the Pool of Bethesda, I couldn't shake the feeling that I needed to talk with Alex again. He had said something in the prayer that had really stood out to me. I wanted to talk to him a little more in-depth. After lunch, I mustered up the courage to ask him if we could talk and he agreed. Honestly, the rest of the story is a whirlwind. We spent the last three days of the trip together talking and getting to know each other. On the plane ride home, we exchanged numbers. Once we got home, we started dating. In six months, we were engaged, and in ten more months, we were married.

I discovered, after we started dating, Alex had experienced a lot of the same moments I had on the trip. He noticed me in the airport but had the same "stop it" moment. He had been praying at the Western Wall for a godly wife at the exact same time I had been praying for a godly husband. During the side hug at the pool, we both had a moment of "we fit perfectly together" but we both had brushed it off at the time. The Lord not only took us on an epic adventure to Israel, but he had used this adventure to bring us together as a couple.

Our relationship was founded on an adventure. It's part of the DNA that makes us who we are. After we got married, we started being very intentional about the adventures we took. Our adventures have all kinds of different aspects to them, but travel is our favorite. There is something about traveling that makes us come alive. Traveling strengthens our marriage. We have traveled alone and with others. We have taken small trips and long trips. We have stayed at fancy hotels and we have camped across the United States. Although all our trips have been different, one thing has been constant. God always shows up and speaks to us in unique and wild ways. He is constantly teaching and growing us as we experience different parts of His creation together.

A little over a year ago, while I was spending time with the Lord, I had a thought pop into my head concerning marriage mentoring. I love being married but I see so many couples that are so unhappy. I wanted to help couples have a great marriage. I didn't know exactly what it would look like, but I wanted to advance the Kingdom by displaying a godly, happy marriage. I spoke with Alex about it and he liked the idea of helping others with their marriage. Again, we didn't know what it would look like or even where to start, but we knew we needed to start. So, we spoke to our friends that are married and asked them if we could just hang out with them on a regular basis and maybe do some mentoring. They agreed, so we started meeting with them once a month. It was such a small step of obedience, but wow did the Father honor it. Keep in mind, we didn't tell anyone what we were doing. This was just between us and the Lord. However, people started approaching us and it was always marriage related. I love the way the Lord sends a confirmation. It was people who had no connection to each other. The people came from several different areas of our life, but the subject was always the same: marriage.

Fast forward a few months, the mentoring was going well, I was watching an Instagram story from my favorite author, Jess Connolly. Her Instagram stories are always so positive and encouraging. As I was watching her story the Lord spoke to me and said, "Why don't you do something like this about marriage? Shed an encouraging and positive light on it." I began to think about the way marriage is presented in our world. It is so negative. Just google marriage and see what happens. There is more bad than good. Marriage is considered more of a prison sentence than a covenant. It is given no value or worth. Again, I spoke with Alex about it. He was completely on board. We mentioned the idea to our mentors and they also agreed it would be a great thing. So, *A Beautiful Adventure Marriage* was born. As I sit and write this, the ministry is just over a year old. We are completely internet based with a blog and social media sites. Our main objective is to shine positivity onto marriage. We want people to realize that marriage is God's idea, it's a good idea, and when done the way it was designed, it can be a beautiful adventure! We are so new to this. Neither of us have ever blogged or ran an online ministry, it has been a process to learn, but we are enjoying it so much.

Not long after we started the ministry page, random people in our lives all started saying the same thing to us. Write a book. The thought had crossed my mind in the past, but I never gave it more than one thought before moving on to something else. To be honest, when people first started talking about it, I continued to brush off the idea. It seemed so big and out of my comfort zone. I didn't feel qualified to write and I sure didn't think I had anything to say that people would want to read. But God didn't stop conveying His message to us! People kept approaching us with the same message- write the book. Again, these people had no connection with each other. I started praying about it and asking God to tell me what I was supposed to write about in this book. It seemed as if the message was clear on what, but not on how. He answered my question with a question. "When did people start saying you should write a book?" I thought about it and it all started happening with the marriage ministry. We started publishing our blogs on *A Beautiful Adventure Marriage* and people started approaching us about a book. I feel as if, at that moment, the Father was just looking at me blinking His eyes with His arms extended out like," Well any more questions, I've made this pretty clear." Being that I'm a type 5 on the Enneagram and 5s need all the detailed information, I did have more questions. I asked Him what I should write about marriage. It's a pretty big topic and one could really go in any direction. The Father always answers, but He makes us participate in the answer sometimes.

On Christmas Day, Alex and I had talked a little about the book and what direction we wanted to take with it. As we were just casually talking about it, I kept thinking about traveling. What if we gave people a guide to having a godly, happy marriage? Marriage is an adventure to go on, but you need guidance to make an adventure successful. That night I couldn't sleep at all. I had a million things going through my mind. I prayed to God for sleep to come. I was so tired and yet so awake. As I lay there, Israel came to mind. I tried again to cut off the thoughts so I could rest. However, I couldn't shake the thought that I needed to remember Israel and how we met. After fighting it, for what seemed like forever, I got up, went to my office, and wrote down what I was thinking. The Lord revealed to me that He had founded our marriage on six words- adventure, blessings, obedience, prayer, and passionate pursuit. I had never thought about it, but maybe that is why Alex and I love adventure so much. It was a foundational stone that our marriage was built upon. I started thinking about everything that goes into our adventures. Alex and I do a lot of prep work when we travel, we are very intentional. We always establish a road map to help guide us to our desired location and back. We research the area we are going to so we can pack accordingly. We typically know a great deal about where we are going and what it has to offer before we get there. All of this brought me to this conclusion. Our adventures are only successful because we put in the work to make them successful. We plan and pace ourselves to arrive happily at our destination. What if we could offer that same help to others to make their marriage successful? What if we created a marriage "guide"? Something people could refer to for guidance on their marriage adventure.

That is exactly what this book is- a "guide" that when followed, will help you have a godly, happy marriage. Marriage was God's idea and it's a good idea. It can be a beautiful adventure. We as a couple, must partner with God and be intentional if this is going to work. We must plan and pace ourselves so we can enjoy the journey and arrive at our destination happily.

I pray this book becomes something you won't only read once but will refer to anytime you need more guidance. Each chapter will offer something needed to help you get further down the road on your marriage adventure. There will be a character trait and practical applications in each chapter that you will need to learn and practice in your relationship. Some chapters may be quick reads just for encouragement and refreshment. You can quickly fill your tank and keep on moving because you are already implementing it. While in other chapters you may have to camp out there and spend some time to really learn something new, apply the concept, and grow from it. There will be chapters you read that may not apply now, but in the future will have to be revisited as different seasons arrive. I encourage you to take all the time you need. Read and re-read as much as is necessary. This is not a weekend getaway, but the adventure of a lifetime. It was meant to be a beautiful one.

Let's get started!

beau·ti·ful

/ˈbyoodəfəl/

adjective

1. pleasing the senses or mind aesthetically.
2. of a very high standard; excellent.

ad·ven·ture

/adˈven(t)SHər,ədˈven(t)SHər/

noun

1. an unusual and exciting experience or activity.
2. engage in an exciting activity, especially the exploration of unknown territory.

PART 1

Get a Plan

CHAPTER 1

PREPARATION FOR THE ADVENTURE

"Most people don't plan to fail; they just fail to plan."
John L Beckley

We had just left Alex's Dad's house. It was Thanksgiving Day 2010. We had known each other for about two weeks, and this was technically our second date. Our first date was a week earlier and had gone very well. We had been talking to each other pretty much every day and I really liked him. Meeting someone before the holidays can be a little tricky. You really don't know if you should invite them to your family events or not, especially when the relationship is so new. For me, it was easy. That year I didn't have any plans for Thanksgiving. Alex had plans on both sides of his family, so He decided to ask me to come to Thanksgiving dinner with his Dad's family. It was a chilly night and we were barely out of the driveway on our way home when I asked Alex this question, "So, what are we exactly?" Maybe it was the turkey that gave me this moment of bravery (or stupidity) but I have never been one to waste time. I figured we might as well have this talk now. Alex thought for a few moments and then told me that he wanted me to be his girlfriend, exclusively. We decided at that moment to commit to dating only each other.

Fast forward six months, May 15th to be exact, Alex tells me that he wants to take me on a picnic after church. He drives me to a little creek in the woods near my house where my Dad used to take me to play when I was a little girl. When we got there, he had everything set up. A little blanket beside the water with sandwiches and fruit. It was perfect in every way. Little did I know, it was Alex's turn to ask me a serious question. We had only been there a few moments when Alex got down on one knee and asked me to marry him. It was my turn to decide if I wanted to commit to this relationship or not. I think you all know what my answer was.

Now, I am not saying that everyone should have this conversation on their second date and be engaged six months later. It worked for Alex and me, but everyone has their own story and own timeline. The point I'm trying to make with these two stories is, there will come a time when you are going to have to decide on whether you are all in. This is a very important decision that needs to be made with a lot of prayer and thought. It's one of the most important decisions of your life. If you decide to go all-in then you need to commit to that decision!

Get Rid of Your Contingency Plan

So, Elijah departed from there and found Elisha the son of Shaphat, while he was plowing with twelve pairs of oxen before him, and he with the twelfth. Elijah went over to him and threw his mantle (coat) on him. He left the oxen and ran after Elijah and said, "Please let me kiss my father and mother [goodbye], then I will follow you." And he said to him, "Go on back; for what have I done to [stop] you?" So, Elisha left him and went back. Then he took a pair of oxen and sacrificed them and boiled their meat with the implements of the oxen [as fuel], and gave the meat to the people, and they ate. Then he stood and followed Elijah and served him.

1 KINGS 19:19-21 AMPLIFIED BIBLE

If we are going to go on this adventure and be happy, we have got to get rid of our contingency plan. Turning back or giving up must be completely off the table. If we say we are all in, then it needs to mean that we are indeed all in! Why is this decision so important? When you commit to something completely, with no intention of quitting, it forces you to make it work. There is no other option.

In 1 Kings we find Elisha working in a field. He is plowing 12 acres of land and is on his last acre. This was not a hobby for him. This was his livelihood. He was working on a big project and was almost finished when Elijah comes and offers him an adventure of a lifetime. What Elisha does next is mind-blowing. Not only does he accept the offer, but he shows that he is all in by burning the plow and killing the oxen. There is no way this prophet thing can't work now because Elisha doesn't have anything to fall back on. Even if he quits and comes back home there is nothing there for him to pick back up. He literally throws a farewell BBQ to his old lifestyle and sets off to make this new adventure work. He got rid of his contingency plan. He was going to be a prophet and that is exactly what happened. Not only did he become a prophet, but he performed double the miracles that Elijah, his mentor, performed. I believe his success as a prophet can be traced back to the "all-in" decision he made.

We need to have this same "all in" moment with our marriages. According to my google search, roughly 50% of marriages end in divorce. That is a staggering number. So how do we help this percentage to go down? We don't get divorced! We need to burn the plow of divorce and move forward knowing this is our only option. There is something very freeing in making the decision to be all in. When you decide divorce is completely off the table, it takes the stress off your marriage. You can focus only on making it work. Alex and I both have divorce in our family line. We knew we would have to be very intentional because the enemy would try to use it against us. So, before we said "I do" we sat down and made a decision. Not only would we never get a divorce, but we would never say the word in reference to our marriage. We didn't stop there. We would also NEVER joke about it. Too extreme, maybe, but we are that serious about it. We have absolutely no contingency plan when it comes to us. This relationship will work because that is the only thing it can do. Now it's up to us whether it will work well or not. Alex and I are happily married and this is our heart's desire for everyone. Unfortunately, there are so many people right now married and miserable. They are not getting divorced, but what they have is not what God intended marriage to be. This, to me, is one of the greatest tragedies. Marriage is a beautiful thing. It can be so life-giving when done correctly but it takes daily work. Getting rid of your contingency plan is a great place to start but you can't stop there; in fact, the work has just begun...

Before we go any further, I think a decision needs to be made. Are you all in? Are you ready to ditch any contingency plan you may have and fully commit to this adventure? Are you ready to do the daily work it takes to produce a healthy, happy marriage? Prayerfully consider these questions because when it comes to your marriage's longevity your response is crucial.

If you're continuing to read this, I am believing that your answer was yes! Congratulations, you have just made one of the greatest decisions of your life. The road ahead may not always be smooth. It may be a little bumpy at times, but my goodness, it's going to be beautiful.

I said earlier that once you make this decision the work is just beginning. So, what should we do next?

Ask the Lord for Guidance

Whenever we travel, if we know anyone that has gone on the same trip, we always ask them for advice. Why? Because they have been there and done that. They have the wisdom we need to make our trip more enjoyable. We've had the best time and eaten some of the best food because of recommendations from other people. We have also not wasted time on things because someone told us it wasn't worth doing. We can do the same thing for our marriages. Let's start by asking the God that created marriage to help us. He has all the wisdom we need and is gracious to extend it to us if we ask.

So, first things first-

Abba,
Marriage was Your idea and it was a good idea. Thank You for blessing us with the gift of marriage and our spouses. Help us to steward this gift well. Be with us on this adventure and give us wisdom as we do this life together. Bless our marriage and help us to be a model of You and the church. Come be with us every day and help us to draw closer to You as we draw closer to each other.

Amen

The One who created marriage is now in it with us! This alone can make your relationship so much better but let's not stop here. The Lord has given us His Word and other great resources to help us along. Let's dive in and start researching ways to have a successful marriage.

Research the Area

I recently did a poll on Facebook with this question, "What do you do to prepare for a trip?". I loved seeing the responses. Some people handle their trips with such detail. Every single step in the process was very intentional and thoroughly thought out. They had a day by day itinerary for the week leading up to the trip and a separate itinerary for the trip itself. While other people didn't put much thought into it at all. They were honest and said they relied on other people to do the planning. They just packed a bag and took off. It was interesting to see all the different ways people prepared (or didn't prepare) to do the same thing. However, as I was reading all the answers one common theme began to form. Everyone researched the destination beforehand. They wanted to know what restaurants were there, what activities were offered, and what hotels were available. Even the people who just packed a bag said they had a person that would handle the research and details. No one I talked to went on a trip completely blind.

Why is the research so important? Well, no one wants to take a vacation and find out that the destination they chose has nothing to offer, right? When we decide to use our hard-earned resources to go on a trip, we want to experience new and exciting things. In short, we want to make new memories we can look back on and enjoy. So why should our marriage adventure be any different? Why should we spend so much time planning for a week's vacation and not take the time to plan for a lifetime together?

So how do we "research the area" when it comes to marriage?

Study Yourself and Your Spouse

Study and do your best to present yourself to God approved, a workman [tested by trial] who has no reason to be ashamed, accurately handling and skillfully teaching the word of truth.
2 TIMOTHY 2:15 AMPLIFIED BIBLE

In this verse, Timothy is not directly talking about marriage, but we can use this verse to help our marriage. Marriage is a gift that has been given to us by God. It was God's idea and it's a good idea. As such we need to steward it well. We need to take care of it and handle it correctly. We can only do this if we study! We can only do this if we take the time to really get to know ourselves, our spouse, and our relationship.

One way we can "research the area" in our marriage is by becoming a lifetime student of ourselves and our spouse. Let's study them and ourselves like we would for a big test. Let's make it our goal to find out everything. That way we can be the best version of ourselves and know about who we married. I'm talking about everything! Let's find out what they like and what they don't like, their strengths and their weaknesses, their personality traits, their favorite ice cream, what conditioner they use, everything! We do so well at learning about our spouses when we are dating. We want to be with them all the time. We think they are totally perfect, and we want to know everything about them. During the dating and engagement period, we are the "teacher's pet". We're not only doing the assignment, but we're asking for extra credit. We are arriving early and staying after class. This is such a fun time. The relationship is new, and you have all the "feels". Unfortunately, for most couples, once the wedding is over the learning stops. Maybe it's because the pressure to "win them over" is off? Maybe we just get lazy? Maybe life just happens, and it's unintentional? Whatever the reason the outcome is the same, unhappy marriages. The sad thing is people think this is a normal occurrence and accept it as such. When Alex and I first got married we heard things like this.

"We can tell y'all are newly married, that will wear off soon."
"All those things you think are cute now will be annoying later."
"One day you are going to realize he/she isn't perfect."

Isn't it sad that instead of encouraging us to continue like we were, people were speaking negativity over us? I'm sure if you are reading this, you have heard the same things or maybe even worse. It's unacceptable that we have gotten to a point where this is the norm.

Perhaps you've bought into the lie that your marriage is only going to get worse as the years go on. Perhaps you've bought into the lie that this is the normal progression a marriage takes and there is nothing you can do about it. Perhaps you have bought into the lie that once you are married the "learning" is over. Let's replace the lies with truth! If you commit to be a lifelong student of your spouse, the "engagement period" does not have to end. Will it change? Yes, but it doesn't have to change for the worse. As you spend time with each other and learn each other, things will shift. You have more information to work with, but it should strengthen your bond and draw you closer together. With a deeper knowledge of your spouse, a deeper love can form, and that deeper love can produce a life-long happy marriage!

We not only need to learn about our spouses, but we need to take the time to learn about ourselves as well. God created us all wonderfully and uniquely. When we understand how we are wired and why we do certain things certain ways, it will help us become better people. When we know our strengths, we can walk in them fully. When we know our weaknesses, we can work on making them stronger. When it comes to learning about ourselves and our spouse, the more we know the more we grow. Our marriages can be better because we are the best version of ourselves.

Knowledge=Personal Growth=Better Marriage

Let's not accept the lie that once we get married things only go downhill. Let's change the normal. Let's make the engagement period last indefinitely in our marriages. How do we do this? I'm glad you asked!

- Date Your Spouse Regularly

To know someone, we must spend one on one time with them on a regular basis. We must talk to them and ask them questions and not assume we already know the answers. I have been with Alex for over nine years and I am still learning things about that man. I don't learn these things about him in large groups of people. I learn these things when it is just the two of us. Dating is something you must be intentional about. Life happens, and if you are not careful, you will look up one day and realize you haven't taken your husband or wife out on a date in months. I know Alex and I have been there. Now, we make it our goal to have at least one date a month. Sometimes we go out and sometimes we stay in. Sometimes we spend money and sometimes we don't. The point is, we set aside time every month to just be together.

Staying connected is the main reason for dating, not going places and spending money. By being intentional about one on one time you will grow closer to your spouse.

- Learn Your Spouse's Love Language. Speak It Daily.

"The Five Love Languages" by Dr. Gary Chapman is a fabulous book that can help you so much in marriage. We all have a primary love language. This is the way that we speak love and receive love from others. Knowing your spouse's love language will help you fully convey how much you care about them. The five love languages are physical touch, acts of service, gifts, words of affirmation, and quality time. I know of a couple that shows how speaking the correct love language will help grow your marriage. Spoiler alert- it's so easy. She is "gifts" and he is "words of affirmation". The husband told me once, "If I give her a Reese cup and a Dr. Pepper and she tells me I am handsome, we are great for the rest of the day." How simple is that?!? The problem is, we speak our language fluently. If we aren't speaking our spouse's language, they may not be receiving your love fully. If he only told her how beautiful she was, and she only gave him gifts it wouldn't work. Yes, we all want to be told something good about ourselves and receive gifts from time to time, but if that's not your primary love language you aren't feeling the full amount of love the other person is trying to give. Speaking the wrong love language is doing twice the work and getting very few results.

11

This one thing can make marriage a lot easier. You can be intentional everyday about saying or doing exactly what speaks love to your spouse.

- Take Personality Tests

The best way to learn about yourself and your spouse is for both of you to take personality tests. There are so many out there right now to choose from. I love personality tests and I have taken several over the last few years. Each one has shown me different aspects of myself and why I do things the way I do. Each one of them has helped me to grow. Recently I have found the Enneagram. It has been so good not only for me personally but for my marriage as well. It has opened my eyes so I can be a better version of myself. It has also helped me to understand Alex better so I can be a better wife to him. The Enneagram is an in-depth personality test that has nine different types. Each type is wired differently and views reality from their own lenses. No type is better than the other. They are just different. Because it's so in-depth, it gives you a clearer picture of yourself and the people around you. Knowing my type and Alex's type has helped us communicate better which has prevented us from having certain arguments and frustrations that we were having before we had this knowledge. We can now see the intentions behind the decisions or actions instead of just jumping to conclusions. I've seen our marriage shift for the better in the last few months just based on this one test. You can take the Enneagram for free at www.yourenneagramcoach. com. This site has a ton of resources to help you know yourself and your spouse better.

The Enneagram is great but take as many personality tests as you can. They all give much-needed insight and wisdom! Be encouraged! The more you know the more you grow. Do the research! Date your spouse. Learn everything you can about them. Learn everything you can about yourself. When you understand yourself and them, your adventure will be a lot smoother. You will avoid certain potholes that cause so much trouble in marriage. There is no point in having a bumpy ride when it can be avoided by taking the time to research!

Secure the Funds and Pack Accordingly

For which one of you, when he wants to build a watchtower [for his guards], does not first sit down and calculate the cost, to see if he has enough to finish it? Otherwise, when he has laid a foundation and is unable to finish [the building], all who see it will begin to ridicule him, saying, 'This man began to build and was not able to finish!'

LUKE 14:28-20 AMPLIFIED VERSION

By researching the area, you are setting yourself up for success. However, you also need to make sure you pack your bag with items that are necessary to make the trip an enjoyable one. If you were to go on a 7-day road trip, but you didn't take clothes, money, or snacks, it would not be very enjoyable. You would probably end up stranded on the side of the road somewhere- dirty, upset, and hungry. The same is true for marriage. By preparing ahead of time for future needs we can have a fun trip and avoid certain potholes other couples may be hitting along the way.

- Marriage Counseling

Alex and I were forced into premarital counseling. I kid you not, our pastor and his wife literally said, "You let us counsel you or we will not marry you." Remember when I said we were engaged within six months of meeting each other? That probably had a lot to do with it. Now I can say, it was one of the best things we have ever done. It forced us to really look at some areas that needed attention both individually and as a couple if our relationship was going to work. Through this counseling, we were packing our bags for success. We took things out of our bag that would not benefit us, and we replaced them with things we would need to make our marriage adventure as smooth as possible. Everyone comes into a relationship with their own baggage. You won't empty your bag of everything you need to during counseling, but it does help to lighten the load. If you're engaged, I highly recommend it. Honestly, I recommend it for anyone who is married. Counseling has a negative stigma on it. People view counseling as a last-ditch effort. From my experience, it can be helpful, even if things are going well. When we were in counseling, we had not had a disagreement yet, much less a full-blown argument. We laugh and tell people that our pastors put us through the wringer during premarital counseling and just to be clear, they did. However, now I see it was such a gift. I see all the times we have implemented what we learned from that counseling and it's mind-blowing. To this day we still use the knowledge that was poured into us. It cleared the path for us so our adventure could be a lot smoother.

My main recommendation here is to seek marriage counseling from a Christian source. Ask your pastor and his wife to counsel you or find a Christian counselor that specializes in marriages. It's important that we find this help from people who believe the same way we do!

- Mentors

Alex and I had been married for a few years when we started praying that the Lord would send us a couple to be our mentors. We were new to marriage and ministry. Honestly, it was a lot. We were struggling to keep everything in its proper place, and to be good stewards of everything the Lord had called us to do. We knew we had been called, and were excited and expectant, but it was a hard season for us. Then the Lord sent us Penny and Andy. When we first met them, we were the youth pastors at our church, and they wanted to volunteer in the youth. This was such a God-ordained moment for us. Not only did they help us in our ministry, but we quickly became good friends. We had no idea how much we needed them in our lives. Since then our friendship has grown into such a beautiful thing. We minister together, travel together, and just do life together. They are the people we call in good times and in bad times. They pray for us, give us godly advice, and call us on our crap. As the years have passed, they have gone from being our friends to our family.

Life is always better in community because that is the way the Lord designed us to live. He never intended for us to do life alone. Yet, so many of us think we have too. The Bible has a lot to say about the importance of seeking out godly advice. Below are just a few verses that touch on this topic.

Where there is no [wise, intelligent] guidance, the people fall [and go off course like a ship without a helm], but in the abundance of [wise and godly] counselors there is victory
PROVERBS 11:14 AMPLIFIED VERSION

Without consultation and wise advice, plans are frustrated, but with many counselors, they are established and succeed.
PROVERBS 15:22 AMPLIFIED VERSION

The wise will hear and increase their learning, and the person of understanding will acquire wise counsel and the skill [to steer his course wisely and lead others to the truth]
PROVERBS 1:5 AMPLIFIED VERSION

Did you notice the common theme in all these verses? We are to seek out wisdom and counsel. It's not something that will just be handed to us without any effort on our part which means we first need to pray and ask God to send us wise counsel. The Lord promises, if we ask for wisdom, He will send it to us.

If any of you lacks wisdom [to guide him through a decision or circumstance], he is to ask of [our benevolent] God, who gives to everyone generously and without rebuke or blame, and it will be given to him.

JAMES 1:5 AMPLIFIED VERSION

The wisdom talked about in this verse may come directly from the Lord in certain situations, but I believe the Lord loves to include His children in His work. So, when we ask God for wisdom it may come in the form of another couple.

Whenever a couple asks me for advice on marriage, I always tell them to put God first. Then, find a married couple to be their mentors. This decision is so important and should not be taken lightly. Below are a few guidelines to follow when you're choosing who should be your mentors.

- Pray about it first.
  - This is not a decision that needs to be made without the Lord. You need to be very intentional with whom you choose. The Lord will be faithful in sending the perfect couple for you but wait on Him to do it. Don't just pick someone out of a crowd and declare them your mentors.

Once you have found someone you think the Lord has sent you, ask yourself these questions.

- Have they been married for a while? Are they happy?
  - You don't need to take advice from someone who is no better off than you are. Find someone with experience. A couple who is doing it right and glean from their wisdom.

- Are they trustworthy?
    - You need to be able to talk to your mentors about real stuff. You can't just tell your business to everyone. You need to be confident that what you tell them stays between them, you, and the Lord.
- Do they have a strong relationship with God and a strong prayer life?
    - I saved the most important one for last. They need to be like-minded with you. In fact, I believe they need to have a stronger relationship with the Lord than you do. You need to be able to grow and learn from them.

Since meeting Penny and Andy, Alex and I have grown in every area. They pray for us and share their wisdom with us daily. I know for a fact we are stronger as a married couple, and as Christians in general, because of their mentorship.

- Money Classes

Another thing our pastors made us do was take a Dave Ramsey money class. This class, like the counseling, was a non-negotiable. I had it in my head this was a short three-week class but at the first meeting it was revealed it was actually thirteen weeks! This class covered everything. Which was great, because Alex and I didn't have anything! We were in debt up to our eyeballs. Alex had a car payment and a student loan. I had eleven maxed out credit cards and no job! What can I say? I was very stylish in college. Unfortunately, several years had passed since college and I was still wearing those same clothes because of the eleven maxed out credit cards and no job. I went into this class a little begrudgingly. To be real, I was embarrassed and overwhelmed by our finances. We wanted to buy a house in town, but I knew looking at the numbers, it wasn't a possibility. This reality just made me want to give up. It seemed so insurmountable.

This class helped change our mindset and our money habits. It gave us hope that being debt-free was possible. But it didn't stop there. It also gave us a plan to make our dreams our new reality.

Our problem was not a lack of money. Our problem was the way we were using money. Money, and the stresses that come with it, are a leading cause of conflict in marriage. Money has caused a few "discussions" between Alex and me even with us trying to accomplish a set goal. So, I can see where it can cause major strife if a couple is not working together. I shudder to think about how we would have handled marriage and finances had we not taken this class before we said I do.

Based off our experience, I encourage you to find a money class. You can take the Dave Ramsey class from the comfort of your own home. They have condensed it down, it isn't 13 weeks anymore, but it covers the same information. If you don't have the margin in your schedule to take a class, there are books and information online. You and your spouse should find a way to learn about money and the proper way of handling it. When it comes to money, you both need to be on the same page to accomplish your goal. Below are just a few starting points to help start the process of getting your finances back on track.

- Tithe (10%)
  - This may seem counterintuitive to tell you to give money away when we're talking about being a good steward of money. However, the Lord has asked us to tithe in the following verses.

Bring all the tithes (the tenth) into the storehouse, so that there may be food in My house, and test Me now in this," says the Lord of hosts, "if I will not open for you the windows of heaven and pour out for you [so great] a blessing until there is no more room to receive it. Then I will rebuke the devourer (insects, plague) for your sake and he will not destroy the fruits of the ground, nor will your vine in the field drop its grapes [before harvest]," says the Lord of hosts. "All nations shall call you happy and blessed, for you shall be a land of delight," says the Lord of hosts.

MALACHI 3:10-12 AMPLIFIED VERSION

If we are not faithful in our tithes, we are not going to be blessed. We must be obedient to God first if we're going to be good stewards of our money. Look closer at verses 11 and 12, if we are faithful to this principle the Lord will not only bless us, but He'll rebuke the devourer (all those little things that pop up and take our money). That's a pretty good deal if you ask me.

Jesus said a lot about money and how to manage it. In the following verses, He tells us, if we can't handle our money appropriately, we won't be able to handle greater things appropriately.

"He who is faithful in a very little thing is also faithful in much, and he who is dishonest in a very little thing is also dishonest in much. Therefore, if you have not been faithful in the use of earthly wealth, who will entrust the true riches to you?

LUKE 16:10-11 AMPLIFIED VERSION

I could tell you several personal testimonies of where God has proven Himself faithful to the principle of tithing. A blessed 90% goes way further than a cursed 100%. Don't believe me? I challenge you to try it for two months. Watch and see what the Lord will do!

- Save (10% or whatever works best)
    - God is very specific about how much he wants us to tithe. He gives us the freedom to do what we want with the other 90%. Saving is so important. It needs to be the next thing we do after we've tithed. I recommend having a set percentage or a set amount you save from

every paycheck. Look at your finances and make your decision based on what you can do.

Why save? I don't know about you, but if we have extra money just lying in our checking account it's easy for us to pull out our debit cards. Soon the extra money is nowhere to be found and typically there isn't anything to show for it. By taking a set amount and putting it into another account (without a debit card) it makes it easier for us not to spend it. With that amount stored away, when we want to travel, have an emergency, or an unexpected expense, we don't have to stress.

Dave Ramsey suggests having at least 500 to 1000 dollars in an emergency fund. You never touch it unless there is an emergency. This was one of the first things Alex and I did after taking the course. It has been so helpful in our marriage. Let me share two personal examples of how having an emergency fund will change a situation.

About 4 years ago total chaos struck at our house in a 24-hour period. Our washer, dryer, and lawnmower all died at the same time. I can't make this up! All of them! We didn't have an emergency fund in place. Because we didn't have the extra money available, we put a washer, dryer, and lawnmower on a credit card. This was such a stressful situation for us. We needed these items, but we knew we would be paying a lot of interest for them since it was going to take time to pay the credit card off. This large amount would negatively affect our credit score and it wouldn't help to buy a house. Alex wanted quality items because they were necessities we would use on a regular basis. I wanted the cheapest items possible because all I could see was the credit card bill. Without an emergency fund, this whole situation brought a lot of stress on our marriage.

About 6 months ago we came home from church to find our whole kitchen flooded. Our refrigerator had died. All the ice and water from the ice maker had melted and was now residing on our floor. This time we had our emergency fund ready. We cleaned up the water, went to Lowes, got a refrigerator and came home! This whole situation was so much easier because of the money we had set aside. The only decision that had to be made was which refrigerator we wanted. Alex wanted an ice maker, I wanted it to be within our emergency fund. It didn't take us long to find one that fit both requirements. There was no stress and no contention on our marriage.

These are just two examples of why having some money put back is so important. It really does take so much stress off your marriage when those random, costly situations pop up. Don't be caught off guard and bring unnecessary stress to your marriage! Be a good steward and save. It may start small and that's perfectly ok! Just start and be faithful in this!

- Spend (80% or whatever is left after tithing and saving)
  o Pay your bills and live off the rest!

Dave Ramsey has a saying "Live like no one else so one day you can live like no one else". What he means by this is to make the sacrifices now with your money so in the future, you will have the money to do what you want to do. If you commit to this process you may have to start telling yourself and others "no".

- No, we can't buy that.
- No, I'm not going to put that on the credit card.
- No, we can't go there.

Saying "no" is never fun. When Alex and I first started this process, we said "no" a lot and can I be real with you- it sucked. It was frustrating and embarrassing. But now, we don't have to say "no" very often. There are still times where we have to decline something, if we can't afford it, but for the most part, we can say "yes". Being able to say "yes" made us see that going through the process of improving our finances was worth it.

It has been 8 years since we took the class. During this time, we have taken other money classes at our church and are currently retaking the Dave Ramsey course online. As your seasons change, so does the way you need to handle your money. We realized, we weren't in the same place now and a refresher would be helpful. We aren't debt-free yet but, let me tell you what has happened since we took that first class. We paid off all our cars, his student loan, and all my credit cards. The only reason we aren't debt-free now, is we were able to finally buy the house we wanted. I don't tell you this to brag but to encourage you. It doesn't matter how bad your finances look right now. It can be better if you put in the work. We must work at this every single day, but it's so worth it. That class taught us how to be good stewards of what the Lord had given us. We would not have our house in town or be in a good financial position had we not taken the money class and learned how to handle our money well.

You can do this. Go through the process- tithe, save, and make wise decisions with your money. Embrace the "no" moments now so you can have the "yes" moments in the future. Rid your marriage of the stresses that come from financial issues.

Let the Adventure Begin

As we come to the end of the first chapter, I feel like I need to close with this statement. None of this will work unless you work it. You must take the wisdom you'll learn from doing these prep steps and apply it <u>every day</u> for it to have any effect on your marriage. Knowledge is great, but the application is where we see change. Apply this knowledge to your relationship and it will improve. If you work through these steps it will pay off. If you want your marriage to be the beautiful adventure the Lord created it to be, you must prepare and do your part! Your marriage is the adventure of a lifetime! Let's keep going!

CHAPTER 2

THE NAVIGATOR (WIFE)

Wives, submit to your own husbands, as to the Lord. For the husband is the head of the wife even as Christ is the head of the church, his body, and is himself its Savior. Now as the church submits to Christ, so also wives should submit in everything to their husbands. Husbands, love your wives, as Christ loved the church and gave himself up for her, that he might sanctify her, having cleansed her by the washing of water with the word, so that he might present the church to himself in splendor, without spot or wrinkle or any such thing, that she might be holy and without blemish. In the same way, husbands should love their wives as their own bodies. He who loves his wife loves himself. For no one ever hated his own flesh, but nourishes and cherishes it, just as Christ does the church because we are members of his body. "Therefore, a man shall leave his father and mother and hold fast to his wife, and the two shall become one flesh. "This mystery is profound, and I am saying that it refers to Christ and the church. However, let each one of you love his wife as himself, and let the wife see that she respects her husband.

EPHESIANS 5:22-33 ENGLISH STANDARD VERSION

As I was preparing to write this book, I wanted to be very intentional with each chapter. I wanted each chapter to be about something that would not only strengthen your marriage but would strengthen you as a child of God as well. I want us to draw closer to God as we draw closer to each other. In my notebook, I drew a picture of the layout of the book. I knew some of the chapters immediately, so I wrote them down. My main struggle was picking the order of the chapters. I knew chapter one would be all about preparation for our adventure, but I struggled with what the topic of chapter two should be. Then it occurred to me, if we don't study God's design for marriage first and foremost our adventure will be bumpy no matter what we do! If we don't know what our role in marriage is, how will we be able to accomplish it?

When you go on a road trip one person drives and the other person helps with the directions, right? If both people are trying to drive, it's chaotic and dangerous. If neither person gets behind the wheel, you don't go anywhere at all. The same is true in marriage. Ephesian 5 tells us the husband is the head of the home and he is called to love his wife well. The wife is to submit to her husband and respect him. Going with our adventure theme, we are going to say the husband is the driver and the wife is the navigator. For a marriage to be successful there needs to be a driver and navigator, and the Lord has already assigned these roles for us. If we will learn what our roles are and perform them according to God's word our trip will be enjoyable. With this in mind, the next two chapters are going to be focused on what God's design for marriage is and practical ways the husband and the wife can stay in their lane and have a happy marriage by honoring God and each other.

Stay in Your Lane

One of the first rules on a road trip is to stay in your lane. If you are swerving all over the road, a head-on collision is going to happen.

However, when you stay in your lane with one person driving and the other person helping to navigate you will arrive at your destination safely. If we look at God's Word, we will find the lanes the Lord wants the husband and the wife to stay in to ensure not only a happy marriage, but one that is blessed by God as well. A marriage that models Christ and His church. You can find a lot about marriage in the New Testament. In Ephesians, Paul talks about the roles the husband and the wife have in the marriage relationship. So, if God has given us this manual, why are so many Christian couples struggling? One reason I have found is we have a distorted view of what Paul is telling us.

The enemy knows how powerful a couple can be when their marriage lines up to God's Word. Because of this, he has done everything in his power to distort God's design. He tells us a husband is to be an iron-fisted dictator of the home, not a gentle, godly leader who provides for and protects his wife. He tells us submission means a lifetime of unappreciated servitude, not a sacred privilege we have been given to lift our husbands up in honor. Sadly, we have taken those lies and ran with them. We have wives reaching over and trying to grab the wheel instead of helping their husbands navigate the trip and as a result crashes are happening. We have husbands that are driving with some serious road rage or have taken their hands off the wheel entirely and as a result, crashes are happening. I would love to report that I never bought into the lies the enemy tells us about these verses; however, I did buy into what he said, and I had a very strong hate for these verses way before I ever met Alex.

A Sacred Privilege

I Will Not Say Obey!

That is exactly what I said to Alex as we were preparing our vows and planning our wedding. I didn't stop there; I went on to tell him I was looking for a husband not a father, so I didn't see any reason to say obey. When would I ever need to "obey him" anyway?

I know. I know. This was not my best moment! Let me explain!

I was raised by a fiercely independent woman and was taught very young I should always be able to take care of myself. My daddy was an amazing man, but he passed away when I was 12. I didn't have any memories of him "leading" our family. I remember my mama taking care of herself and me with very little outside help. I also saw some very unhealthy marriages around me where the men were very domineering, and the women were just along for the ride. I made up my mind very early. I was not going to be treated like a doormat and I would never let a man tell me what to do. I had heard sermons on Ephesians 5 and submission, but it seemed unfair and outdated. I had no desire or plans to be submissive, to anyone. I can see now how incredibly rude and "out of nowhere" this must have seemed to Alex. He had never given me any reason to say this. I was basing this whole conversation, not on what I had seen in Alex, but my own preconceived notions of how he would act as soon as he became my husband. At that moment, Alex had every right to lose his temper, but I remember how chill he was about it. He just looked at me and told me I could say or not say whatever I wanted in the vows and we went on planning everything out. Our wedding day came and went. I didn't say obey!

It wasn't until several months after our wedding that he told me how much my statement had hurt him. He told me he knew I said it because of what I had seen in others, but he had never given me a reason to project that on him. That was eye-opening to me. I started thinking about submission and wondering if maybe I had a misconception of what it meant. I started watching how Alex treated me, both in public and in private, and how he led with such a gentle spirit. I saw how he gave me grace when I didn't deserve it. How he did things with and for me just because he loved me. I wanted to be a godly wife because of how good Alex was to me. I really started studying what it meant to be submissive and started trying my very best to walk it out.

What I discovered, through this time of studying, was I did have a wildly incorrect understanding of what it meant to be a submissive wife. I had believed a lie! I've come to realize, when we do things the way the Lord intended them to be done, life is so much better. I learned submission doesn't mean a life of servitude and mistreatment. I learned being a submissive wife is a beautiful thing and a sacred privilege. The Lord's definition of submission was very different from what the enemy had led me to believe. The enemy wants us to believe being submissive is a bad thing. For way too long, I believed the lie. You may be believing the lies the enemy is telling as well. I want to share with you what I learned about Ephesians 5 and expose the enemy for what he is- a liar.

Wives, submit to your own husbands, as to the Lord. For the husband is the head of the wife even as Christ is the head of the church, his body, and is himself its Savior. Now as the church submits to Christ, so also wives should submit in everything to their husbands.
EPHESIANS 5:22-24 ENGLISH STANDARD VERSION

You should know up-front... I'm a nerd. I love to look up definitions of words to get a better understanding of them. After I started studying these verses, the first thing I noticed was God told me to do two things as a wife. My role was to submit to Alex and to respect him. I went to google, and I looked up the definition for those two words!

- Submit means- *accept or yield to the will of another person*
- Respect means- *a feeling of deep admiration for someone or something*

Staying with the adventure theme, this is my definition of what our role is as a wife.

We are the navigators of the trip. We are there for assistance and encouragement. We help the driver make decisions which will get us further down the road. However, we are not the driver. They are. We're there for support in any decision that needs to be made. Our opinions are important. But, at the end of the day, it's the driver who makes the final decision. We are navigators, not back seat drivers- there is a difference. We are to give our encouragement and assistance with a gentle spirit, not a domineering one. Without the navigator, the driver could get lost. Without our encouragement, they could be tempted to give up. Without our help, the trip would be harder for the driver and they would tire more easily. We are the navigators. We are an integral part of God's design for marriage.

Our role is so important ladies. The enemy wants us to believe the opposite. He wants you to believe you can't do it or shouldn't do it. But what if I told you it's not as hard as it may seem? There might even be a chance you've been doing it all along.

You've Had the Power All Along

Does anyone else love the "Wizard of Oz" has much as I do? One of my favorite scenes is at the very end when Dorothy believes all hope is lost. The hot air balloon has floated away and with it her ability to go back home to Kansas. It's in this moment of despair that Gilda drops some wild and beautiful truth on Dorothy. She tells her she has had the power inside of her all along to go back home, but she had to learn it for herself. It was a power she had to discover herself. No one could tell her. I believe the same is true for us wives! We have the power within us, because of Jesus, to be the wives He has called us to be. We have the power within us, because of Jesus, to be the wives our husbands need and deserve. You have it inside of you already, you just have to believe it for yourself.

Take a trip back in time with me ladies, to when you and your spouse first met. How did you treat him? I bet you couldn't wait to see him or talk to him on the phone. He was the smartest, strongest, and the hottest man you had ever seen right?! You thought he was the best thing ever. I bet you told everyone about him! You did things just because you knew you would be together. You did things just because he wanted to do them. Why did you do all that? Why did you talk highly of him and do things with him? Because he was the best and you were so in love, right? You were honoring him and submitting and didn't even realize it. The problem is we tend to stop doing those things after marriage. The new wears off, and the fuzzy feelings go away, and with it goes the submission and respect.

Now you may be thinking, "Well, he deserved it then. He was doing all these awesome things for me! He doesn't do those things anymore so why should I act the same way I did?"

Good question! Let me give you the answer by looking at a lady in the Bible you may already know.

Let's go way back to the Old Testament where we find Abraham and Sarah. You've got to love Sarah. She had her moments of crazy, (who can forget that whole Haggai scandal) but if you really look at Sarah you can see she had a deep respect for Abraham. I mean, Abraham got up one morning and told her God was telling him to go to "a place I will show you" and she followed him. The Bible doesn't say she asks any questions or even fought him on this. She just packed her bags and went with him. She had to be a "ride or die" kind of girl and I can dig that! She had to have been a brave woman with an amazing sense of adventure. But there was something Sarah wanted desperately- a baby- and even though God had promised them it would happen the "going home outfit" was still hanging in the closet. By the time the angels showed up and told Abraham he was about to be a dad, both were very old and had all but given up on their dream. Let's jump into the story right there.

And they said to him, where is Sarah your wife? And he said, [She is here] in the tent. The Lord said, I will surely return to you when the season comes round, and behold, Sarah your wife will have a son. And Sarah was listening and heard it at the tent door which was behind Him. Now Abraham and Sarah were old, well advanced in years; it had ceased to be with Sarah as with [young] women. [She was past the age of child-bearing]. Therefore, Sarah laughed to herself, saying, After I have become aged shall I have pleasure and delight, my lord (husband), being old also?

GENESIS 18:9-12 AMPLIFIED VERSION

Did you catch it? Sarah called Abraham "lord" a term of respect, but she said it to herself. You may be thinking, "Ok, what's your point?!" She respected Abraham so much she showed him respect and honor even when no one would see or hear her. She didn't treat him one way in public and another way in private. She always gave him respect! Why did she do this? She was talking to herself; she could have called him anything and no one (besides God) would have heard her.

She did it because he was her husband and for that one reason alone, he deserved respect and honor. Was Abraham perfect all the time? No! Remember the time he told her to tell Pharaoh she was his sister? Yeh, Abraham had his faults too, but Sarah chose to honor him anyway. She held him in a position of honor because he was her husband.

LADIES- please grab a hold of this and run with it! Your husband deserves respect and honor simply because he is YOUR husband. He shouldn't have to do anything to earn it. He should simply receive it! We're going to talk about what the Lord said to the husbands in the next chapter, but for now, let's just say they have a lot of responsibility that comes with the position they hold. Let's show them our support and respect instead of just demanding more from them. Are they perfect? No, but if you're using that as an excuse to disrespect your man, can I just gently nudge you out of your holiness bubble long enough to say, you're not perfect either! Will they make mistakes? Yes, but use those moments as opportunities to extend the grace which has so lavishly been extended to you. They need us to be a soft place to land. Someone who will speak life into them not death. And it's my experience, if you will give them that soft place and those encouraging words, they will dust themselves off from any mistakes and come back stronger and better than ever. If you treat him like he is the best man ever, he will act like the best man ever! It's time for us to lose the excuses as to why we don't want to be submissive and start being the wife the Lord has called us to be.

So, how do we do this whole submit and respect thing? I'm a practical girl who likes practical steps I can do every day. In this book, I will never tell you to do something without giving you ways to do it. Let's look at a few ways we can be submissive and respectful to our husbands daily.

Practical Ways to Submit and Respect Your Husband

We must make up our minds that the enemy is a liar and we aren't going to buy into those lies anymore. We must make up our minds we're going to be respectful to our husbands and submit to him for the simple fact that he is our husband. We're not going to wait for him to "deserve" it and we're not going to let our submission be contingent on what kind of day he is having. Take a moment and let this sink in. We're choosing today to be submissive because this is what the Lord told us to do! We're standing on the truth that submission is not a burden, but a privilege given to us by our sweet Daddy God. It's a power within us. It can be used for the betterment of our marriages and the glory of God. It's a good thing! Are you still with me? Good! Below are some things we can do to become the Ephesians 5 wife.

- Speak Well of Him

Our words need to be life-giving when it comes to our husbands. What does that mean? It means, not only are you going to speak highly of him <u>to him,</u> but you're going to speak highly of him <u>to others</u>. Alex and I made an agreement before we got married. We would never say anything negative about each other to other people. That means no one knows if we have an argument. We don't put it on Facebook, and we don't go to our families and friends so they will take our sides. We don't make derogatory comments about each other in public or make jokes at the expense of the other. We choose to say things that build the other up. I make it a point every day to say something uplifting to Alex and he does the same to me.

Brag on your man ladies! He has good qualities- focus on them instead of the negative ones. Find someone and tell them something good about your husband. At some point, it will get back to him and he will be encouraged, and you will be reminded that he is a good man. We can lose our perspective sometimes in life. We get bogged down with the stresses of the everyday routine and we tend to forget certain things, like the fact that our husbands are a gift from God or the fact we prayed for them and chose them! We need to remind ourselves, ladies, that he is a good gift with so many good qualities and focus on those. If you will be intentional about reminding yourself of the good things about your husband, you'll find his good qualities far outweigh the bad ones. When this happens, speaking well of him will start to come naturally for you.

- Honor His Request

Do things just because he asks you to do them. Do things you know he would enjoy with no strings attached. Do you know what his favorite meal is? Cook it. Is there something he does you can do for him to lighten his load? Do it. Is there something he wants to be done a certain way? (nothing legally or morally wrong of course) Why not do it his way? By doing these little things on a regular basis you are showing him respect. You are showing him you value his opinion and his position as your husband. The enemy will try and lie to you and make you believe you'll just become a doormat if you put his request first. I know this to be true, because the enemy still tries this lie on me anytime I put Alex above myself. Please don't believe this lie, friends! Showing this respect doesn't undermine your position as his wife. It just acknowledges your care for him. It shows your husband his opinion matters to you and you care about what he cares about. The enemy wants you to believe if you're not selfish you will be overlooked or left out. Really the opposite is true. Selfishness can destroy marriage so quickly if left unchecked. Practice being selfless with your husband. The Lord sees you, friends, and so will your husband as you honor him well.

- Do Not be Historical

Never bring up old fights or past mistakes. No, he's not perfect, but neither are you girlfriend! We need to forgive and walk in that forgiveness. We have all been forgiven of so much from the Lord. Jesus never brings up our past. He forgives and works with us so we can become a better person. We need to extend this same grace to our husbands. Let him off the hook! Don't hold him to some unrealistic or uncommunicated expectations. Show him grace liberally and consistently. If you're quick to forgive him and then move on it will make your husband way more receptive to changing areas that need changing. No one likes to be reminded of a time where they fell short. Bringing the past up just to prove a point will not be helpful to your marriage. Extending forgiveness liberally will.

- Ask Him to Help You be Respectful

This is a good one, ladies, but a hard one as well. Sit down with your husband and ask him point-blank what areas of respect you are good at and what areas need work. The trick is to take the good and keep on rocking it, but to also take the bad (without making excuses for it) and do the work needed to improve that area. Respect is not "respect" if it's not being received by the other person. I did this with Alex a few months ago. I thought for sure he would have told me my good qualities first, but he didn't. That's right, he started out with what I needed to improve. Can I be real? It stung! My first reaction was to start going over all the reasons why I didn't need to improve those areas. It took all the willpower I had to sit there and hear what Alex had to say without saying anything in return. When he was finished, I took a deep breath and said, "Ok, I'll try my best to improve those areas."

Oh friends, don't miss this! It was hard. I didn't like hearing things about myself that needed improvement. Everything inside of me wanted to be defensive. But then, when I didn't say anything else or interrupt him with all my crazy excuses, Alex then went on to tell me how I respected him well. I really enjoyed that part. It spurred me on. I knew the things I was doing well so I could continue them. I also knew the areas I need to focus on going forward. That one conversation, although hard, has been life-giving for me. It opened my eyes to the way Alex defines and receives respect. Do you know what your husband's definition of respect is and how he receives it? I didn't until we had this conversation and going forward, I don't have to guess. I can focus my full attention on respecting Alex in the ways he receives them.

Now, are we going to have that conversation again? Yes, we will have it several times during the course of our marriage if I'm going to continue to respect him well. Remember marriage is the adventure of a lifetime, not a weekend getaway! People change as life goes on. We need to be receptive to those changes. That's why being a lifetime student of your spouse is so important.

Those are just four simple ways I started submitting and respecting Alex. They helped me so much. I hope they do the same for you. Use these as starting points but get creative and find new ways to speak "respect" to your husband. Some days will be easy. Some days will be hard. But I encourage you, be obedient to what the Lord has asked you to do. Remember, He didn't tell us to submit conditionally. He told us to submit in all things (that line up according to His Word.). This may be very hard if your husband isn't being obedient to what the Lord is asking him to do, but remember, you don't have to answer for your husband. You answer for yourself. The Lord honors obedience. You will be inviting God and all His blessings into your marriage when you're walking in accordance with His Word. And when you invite the Lord in, all bets are off. There is no limit to what He can do in and through a wife walking in obedience.

The Power of an Obedient Wife

"Things which the eye has not seen and the ear has not heard, And which have not entered the heart of man, All that God has prepared for those who love Him [who hold Him in affectionate reverence, who obey Him, and who gratefully recognize the benefits that He has bestowed]."

1 CORINTHIANS 2:9 AMPLIFIED VERSION

The enemy really wants us to believe submission is a sign of weakness and servitude, but quite the opposite is true. We've been given such power in our relationship when we walk this principle out in our everyday lives. We have the power to build our husbands up and spur them on. We have the power to encourage them as a husband, but also as a mighty man of God. We have the power to partner with them as they make hard decisions. We have the power to turn them to the Lord if they're lost.

In the same way, you wives, be submissive to your own husbands [subordinate, not as inferior, but out of respect for the responsibilities entrusted to husbands and their accountability to God, and so partnering with them] so that even if some do not obey the word [of God], they may be won over [to Christ] without discussion by the godly lives of their wives, when they see your modest and respectful behavior [together with your devotion and appreciation—love your husband, encourage him, and enjoy him as a blessing from God].

1 PETER 3:1-2 AMPLIFIED VERSION

For in this way in former times the holy women, who hoped in God, used to adorn themselves, being submissive to their own husbands and adapting themselves to them; just as Sarah obeyed Abraham [following him and having regard for him as head of their house], calling him lord. And you have become her daughters if you do what is right without being frightened by any fear [that is, being respectful toward your husband but not giving in to intimidation, nor allowing yourself to be led into sin, nor to be harmed].

1 PETER 3:5:6 AMPLIFIED VERSION

These verses tell us submission is so important that our husbands could be saved simply because of our respectful and submissive behavior. Did you catch that? They could turn toward the Lord by our behavior, not our words. We don't have to preach at our husbands, or "change" them. We don't have to run all over them. We just need to be the respectful and submissive wife the Lord called us to be. Now that is some wild and beautiful stuff! And there is our girl Sarah again! Did her moment of unheard respect matter? I think this verse proves it did. Was Sarah overlooked and mistreated because she chose to honor her husband? I don't think so! Not only is the Lord acknowledging her unspoken respect to Abraham. He is telling us to be like her! Thousands of years later and we are still talking about this one moment of beautiful submission she displayed! Sarah wasn't overlooked. Sarah wasn't a doormat. She was fully seen, fully loved, and fully acknowledge for her obedience. How powerful is that!?!

To Love, Honor, and Obey

Let me close this out by finishing the story I started at the beginning of this chapter. After I dug into Ephesians 5, I realized the true meaning of submission. I had been believing a lie. Submission wasn't a bad word to rebel against, but a Biblical principle to be embraced. I saw submission for what it really was- a powerful, sacred privilege I had been given to help Alex navigate this life by submitting to him and respecting him. Once I made this discovery, I surprised Alex on our one-year anniversary by rewriting my vows to him. I apologized for my shortcomings in this area and recommitted to be the wife he deserved. I laugh, and tell people all the time, my husband had to teach me to be submissive. That's the truth. It was only because Alex chose to be the husband the Lord called him to be that I became the wife the Lord had called me to be. The Lord honored his obedience by piercing my heart.

Since I began studying this principle and started applying it to our marriage the trip has been a lot smoother. We're not swerving all over the road because I'm not fighting him for the wheel. We still hit a few potholes every now and then, but we try hard to extend grace and keep making our way down the road. The enemy still tries to make me believe lies about submission and respect. The lies are a lot easier to spot now. However, I must continually remind myself what the truth is and walk in it. We are both a work in progress, but it's a lot easier now that both of us are trying to work together- Alex driving and me navigating.

You can do this, ladies! Now let's talk to those drivers!

CHAPTER 3

THE DRIVER (HUSBAND)

Wives, submit to your own husbands, as to the Lord. For the husband is the head of the wife even as Christ is the head of the church, his body, and is himself its Savior. Now as the church submits to Christ, so also wives should submit in everything to their husbands. Husbands, love your wives, as Christ loved the church and gave himself up for her, that he might sanctify her, having cleansed her by the washing of water with the word, so that he might present the church to himself in splendor, without spot or wrinkle or any such thing, that she might be holy and without blemish. In the same way, husbands should love their wives as their own bodies. He who loves his wife loves himself. For no one ever hated his own flesh, but nourishes and cherishes it, just as Christ does the church because we are members of his body. "Therefore, a man shall leave his father and mother and hold fast to his wife, and the two shall become one flesh. "This mystery is profound, and I am saying that it refers to Christ and the church. However, let each one of you love his wife as himself, and let the wife see that she respects her husband.

EPHESIANS 5:22-33 ENGLISH STANDARD VERSION

The last chapter was all about the ladies and the instructions the Lord gave the wives. It seems like we hear an awful lot in the church about what the Lord said to the ladies, but very seldom do we hear what the Lord said to the men. In fact, I heard so little about what the Lord says to men that I honestly thought the above verses were the only time He spoke to husbands at all. As I was studying on submission, I realized He said way more to the husbands than He did the wives. I always saw my role as a wife as being so unfair. I was told to submit, and he was told only to love. When you look at it at face value (and with the wrong definition of submit and love might I add) it seems a little unbalanced. It wasn't until I fully understood what the Lord was saying that I realized the men have a huge responsibility.

Not only have they been called to love their wives, but they have also been told how they are supposed to love them and what will happen if they don't obey that call. We will dive deeper into that shortly but first, let me say this, I have a deep respect for the husbands now. For those of you who are walking this out! You da man! For those of you who are trying your best every day! You da man! For those of you who are just now hearing about this, learn all you can and pray. The Lord will help you with this and just for good measure... you da man! It's my prayer that what follows will help you all become the godly husbands the Lord has called you to be. In this chapter, Alex is going to share his own journey in walking out this call, explain what it means to "love like Christ loves the church", and walk you through some practical steps in how to go about it daily. You can do this, men! Let's get started!

Get A Plan

My name is Alex Payne, and I am a planner. In fact, one of the first things Tara remembers hearing me say to someone when we met in Israel was," I have a plan". As you already know, Tara and I love to travel. Whenever we have chosen our destination, I go into plan mode. I love to look at all the available routes and choose which one is best for us. I plan gas stops and bathroom breaks. It's a highly mathematical process that I love. Tara laughs at how thorough I am, but through my process, she has learned I will get us to where we're going, not only safely, but in good time. Because of the trust that has been built between us, she knows she can sit back and enjoy the trip. She trusts me because I have shown her multiple times, I will lead us to where we are going. Tara trusts me so well now she never plans the route at all! She just knows I am going to take care of it. Usually once we get in the car, she falls asleep. She is never a back-seat driver. Now, this trust didn't just happen on its own. It came with time and consistency and having a plan!

I have found there are a lot of parallels between marriage and traveling. In our marriages, we need to have a plan. We need to know where we are going and be able to make sure our families arrive at our destination safely and provided for. Tara doesn't follow me because I force her too. She follows me because I've shown her, I'm a trustworthy driver. That only happened because I consistently had a plan and executed it. As her husband, I need to be the same way in our marriage.

So how do we do this? How do we get a plan together and start executing it in a way which will build this trust? I believe the first thing we must do is pick a destination together. Hopefully, by now you have made up your mind that you're in this for the long haul. So, our destination is pretty easy to figure out, but it's still a discussion that needs to happen between you and your spouse. We want to be happily married to the same person for the rest of our lives, right? Tara and I say our destination is... to grow ridiculously old together. We want to be the old couple you see shuffling around together. We came up with this by sitting down together and talking about it. The driver and the navigator have got to communicate about the destination. If not, you could end up going in two completely different directions.

The trip will be much easier if both people agree on the destination and are working together to get there. A vacation is doomed to fail if the husband thinks they are going to the mountains and the wife thinks they are going to the beach. In this scenario, one or both are going to be frustrated and disappointed. We understand this when planning a trip, but we seem to forget this when it comes to marriage. Every marriage is going somewhere, the trick is to arrive at the same place together and actually be happy about it. That's why communicating about this now is so important. What works for vacations can work for your marriage as well. Tara and I sit down and plan where we want to go. We are both part of the decision. We did the same with our marriage.

Now at this point, you may be saying, "If I am the driver, why don't I just make the decision where we're going and tell my wife?" As the driver, you are the one that makes the ultimate decisions, however, a good driver uses all his resources to arrive at the destination. Genesis 2:18 says, *"Then the LORD God said, "It is not good for the man to be alone. I will make a helper who is just right for him"*. God never intended us to do this on our own. In fact, He flat out says in this verse it's not good for us to be alone. He gave us a helper for a reason-for help! Let's use the help we have so graciously been given. Sit down with your wife, let her be a part of the process. The inclusion of your wife doesn't diminish the position you've been given. It just gives you the help the Lord knew was needed. When you work together as a team, things just go more smoothly.

Now that you and your navigator are on the same page, let's look at exactly what the driver is supposed to do according to the Word of God.

Love like Christ Loves the Church

Husbands, love your wives [seek the highest good for her and surround her with a caring, unselfish love], just as Christ also loved the church and gave Himself up for her

EPHESIANS 5:25 AMPLIFIED VERSION

Ephesians 5 tells us we are the head of the household. Like I said earlier we are the drivers. We have a responsibility to make decisions that will get us and our families to our destination. Our main objective according to the above verse is to love our wives as Christ loves the church. I want to dive into what that means exactly. We can be the drivers in two different ways. We can be domineering, harsh, and have a lot of road rage or we can drive with a gentle, loving spirit, and make the trip enjoyable for everyone. Either way, we will get to a destination. However, the way we decide to drive will determine the condition our families and ourselves are in when we get there and whether we will arrive at the same destination together. We have the power to not only arrive, but to set the tone for the entire trip.

We live in a society that uses the word "love" a lot. We love our wives, but we also love candy! I think we can all agree, we're not talking about the same kind of love here, right? However, because of our overuse of the word, it's easy to not have a great understanding of what it means to "love" something. When you only view love by our society's overuse of it our calling seems so easy, "love your wife as Christ loved the church". However, to do that we have to really look at how Christ loved the church. Christ didn't love the church only when she was having a good day. Christ didn't love the church only when she had her act together. Christ didn't love the church only when she loved Him back. Christ didn't love the church only on the days that He felt like it. His love for the church was completely unconditional and unselfish. Christ pursued the church as she rejected Him. Christ pursued the church as she did everything in her power to make things difficult. Now that is some powerful love. Our culture tells us you only love someone based on how they love you. If they love well, you love well. If they reject, you reject. This is not Christ's love. The church constantly rejected Him, and He still responded in love and care. He decided every day to love the church and take care of her. This is what we are called to do with our wives. Regardless of how she is acting, or the day she is having, we are to make a daily decision to love her and take care of her. Let's look at the different ways Christ showed His love for the church and how that translates to us as husbands.

- Christ loves the church by leading her to the Father

Jesus said to him, "I am the [only] Way [to God] and the [real] Truth and the [real] Life; no one comes to the Father but through Me. If you had [really] known Me, you would also have known My Father. From now on you know Him and have seen Him."

JOHN 14:6-7 AMPLIFIED VERSION

As the driver, it's our responsibility to spiritually lead our wives and family well. We need to constantly lead them to the Father and His Word. We need to make sure our wives are spiritually provided for by making the decision to attend church regularly together, join small groups, and minister together whenever possible. This needs to be a standard in your marriage, not a decision that is made every Sunday morning based on feelings.

Tara and I go to church every Sunday and Wednesday. We don't even talk about the possibility of not going. It has become a part of our weekly rhythm. Because of this decision, we are both being fed spiritually. Because of this decision, we can talk about the service and the sermon together afterward. It not only grows our connection to God but grows our connection with each other as we share what we have learned in church. By being consistent, we have had the ability to make new friends and get plugged into small groups and other ministries. This has given us opportunities to make close relationships with other couples. This helps us spiritually because we gain wisdom from those couples that are like-minded with us. Someone once told me you can't get water from an empty glass. This is so true, and the same principle applies to us men. We can't lead our wives to the Father if we aren't heading in His direction. We must be spiritually filled so we can, in turn, pour into our wives, families, and others around us.

If we're going to have a good marriage both people must be in step with the Father. If we, as husbands, are not making this a priority it will cause problems in our marriage that are easily avoidable.

- Christ loves the church by praying for her

"I do not pray for these alone [it is not for their sake only that I make this request], but also for [all] those who [will ever] believe and trust in Me through their message, that they all may be one; just as You, Father, are in Me and I in You; that they also may be one in Us, so that the world may believe [without any doubt] that You sent Me. I have given to them the glory and honor which You have given Me, that they may be one, just as We are one; I in them and You in Me, that they may be perfected and completed into one, so that the world may know [without any doubt] that You sent Me, and [that You] have loved them, just as You have loved Me.

JOHN 17:20-23 AMPLIFIED VERSION

We should pray with and for our wives daily. Covering your wife in prayer is one of the most powerful things you can do. We have an enemy whose sole job is to steal, kill, and destroy. He wants us to get off course and lose our way. I believe there are very few things on this planet more powerful than a couple that prays for and with each other. There is a unity formed through prayer that can change the world. The enemy knows this, so he tries every day to cause division. One way we can stay on track and unified is by linking up with God in prayer.

By making prayer a daily part of your marriage, you're inviting God to partner with you. Even the best driver needs GPS sometimes. Prayer is our spiritual GPS. It helps us to see what is ahead, avoid traffic jams, and gives us wisdom for the detours that may arise. When we use our spiritual GPS, the chances of us getting off course will be reduced dramatically. Let's think about that for a moment. By praying for our wives and our marriage, we are inviting the God that created marriage to help us. We are inviting the God that created us and our wives to help us. And here is the kicker- He wants to help us! He knows all and wants to extend this wisdom to us for our benefit and for the furtherment of His Kingdom. James 1:5 says, *"If any of you lacks wisdom, you should ask God, who gives generously to all without finding fault, and it will be given to you."* At the beginning of this chapter, I said we should use all our resources. This verse tells us of a resource that is completely at our disposal. All we must do is invite God in and ask for help and He will come and help us!

When it comes to marriage and just life in general, you can never pray too much! Invite God into your marriage daily and see the transformation take place.

- Christ loves the church by providing for her

But God clearly shows and proves His own love for us, by the fact that while we were still sinners, Christ died for us.
ROMANS 5:8 AMPLIFIED VERSION

We have the awesome responsibility to be a provider for our families. The verse above talks about how Christ provided eternal life for us by going to the cross. Thankfully, I don't think we'll ever be asked to be crucified for our wives, but I do believe we need to take up our cross to provide for them daily. What do I mean by "take up our cross to provide"? I mean we must make daily decisions to do things that would be beneficial to our families. It may mean doing things you don't want to do. We know by the way Jesus prayed at the Garden of Gethsemane that He didn't want to go through the suffering; however, He chose to do it so we could be with Him. He did it for our benefit. We as husbands need to do the same thing for our wives.

Tara loves to feel secure. I think this is a desire every woman has. We can help provide that security. There are several ways we can provide security to our wives. One way I provide this security for Tara is by working a job that gives us the money we need for our everyday lives. I enjoy my job, but there are some days (like everyone on the face of the planet) where I just don't want to go to work. On those days, I must make the decision to go anyway. I must go against my feelings and do the things that need to be done to benefit my family. There are other occasions when I must put my wants on hold for our needs. These times are never fun because no one likes to deny themselves, but it's in those moments we get to be like Jesus! Jesus put our need for a Savior above His desire to not suffer. Now, I'm not comparing my going to work to Jesus dying on the cross. There is nothing on this planet that is comparable to what Jesus has done for us. What I do want to point out though, is there are times we must sacrifice for the betterment of our family. In those moments, we get to walk out the sacrificial love Jesus modeled for us. Jesus is and will always be the source of our ultimate provision, but we get to partner with Him and help provide for our wives.

When we provide for our wives it takes stress off our marriage. Money isn't the only thing we get to provide. We get to provide support, affection, strength, and companionship. There are times our wives just need us. They need our presence and nothing else. As I stated earlier, I'm a planner. Since I usually have a plan, I like to fix things. I have found, sometimes Tara doesn't want me to fix it. She just wants me to listen to her or hug her. I get to provide for her by simply giving her a listening ear or a loving embrace. A lot of the time, what we can provide doesn't cost us a thing, just a little time.

I encourage you today, observe your wife. What's something she needs that you can provide today? Is it a loving touch, a listening ear, something material, or help opening a jar? Remember, Jesus is our ultimate provision; however, if it's in your power to provide, be her provision today.

- Christ loves the church by protecting her

And Jesus entered the temple [grounds] and drove out [with force] all who were buying and selling [birds and animals for sacrifice] in the temple area, and He turned over the tables of the moneychangers [who made a profit exchanging foreign money for temple coinage] and the chairs of those who were selling doves [for sacrifice].

MATTHEW 21:12 AMPLIFIED VERSION

Everyone likes to portray Jesus as this meek and mild servant, which is what He was, but if you read the above verse you will see Jesus had a passionate zeal when it came to protecting His bride. He loved His bride (the church) and when He saw people taking advantage of her, He got mad and started flipping tables! He saw a problem and went into action to rid the church of what was hurting it. I believe we need to be just as passionate when it comes to protecting our brides.

There are several ways we can protect our wives. If you're anything like me, you would have no problem flipping a table or two if you saw someone hurting your wife in any way. I have flat out told Tara, the day I see someone hurt her will be the day she will have to bail me out of jail. I am extremely serious about that. I would take care of any physical harm when it comes to her. But let's look at another muscle we can flex to help protect our wives- our tongues.

The Bible has a lot to say about the power of our words. Below are just a few examples from the book of Proverbs.

A soothing tongue [speaking words that build up and encourage] is a tree of life, but a perversive tongue [speaking words that overwhelm and depress] crushes the spirit.
                                    Proverbs 15:4 Amplified Version

For lack of wood the fire goes out, and where there is no whisperer [who gossips], contention quiets down.
                                    Proverbs 26:20 Amplified Version

A soft and gentle and thoughtful answer turns away wrath, but harsh and painful and careless words stir up anger.
                                    Proverbs 15:1 Amplified Version

Death and life are in the power of the tongue, and those who love it and indulge it will eat its fruit and bear the consequences of their words.
                                    Proverbs 18:21 Amplified Version

These verses make it very clear our words hold great power. We can use words to build up or tear down. We can use our words to protect our wives or harm them. How do you speak to your wife? Are you gentle or harsh? How do you talk about your wife to others? Are you talking about her attributes or exposing her shortcomings? The words we speak about our wives are just as important as the words we speak to them. In the next section we are going to dive a little deeper into what happens when we are harsh to our wives. So, let's take this time to focus on how we speak about them to others.

Tara and I made a promise before we got married that we would never talk about each other in a negative way to other people. We would only say positive things about each other in public. This is one way I get to protect her. She knows her name is safe with me. By doing this one thing I am protecting her reputation and her position as my wife. According to Proverbs 15, my words have the power to give life or crush the spirit. I don't want to crush Tara in front of other people. I don't want her constantly worried about what I'm saying about her either. I want to use my words to protect not destroy.

We have an enemy that wants to destroy marriages. By speaking positively, I'm not only protecting Tara, but I'm also protecting our marriage. I'm not giving the enemy any ammunition to use against us. Do we both have shortcomings? Of course, we are two imperfect people. However, we will not grow any closer to each other or to the Father if we choose to expose those shortcomings to others.

I encourage you today to check your words. Flex the muscle that has such great power. If this is something you have a problem with sit down and have a discussion with your spouse. Decide to start fresh and not speak negatively going forward. Be passionate about using your words to protect your wife and your marriage.

Active or Passive?

We are to love our wives daily by leading them to the Father, praying with and for them, providing for them, and protecting them. Love is not a noun; it's a verb. It's meant to be active and alive. I encourage you today, men, do a checkup on your love. Is it active and moving or has it grown passive? If it has grown passive, today is the day to start again. Today is the day to actively love your wife. I recently had a husband to tell me the last month of his marriage had been the best it had been in a long time. I ask him what had changed about it. He told me he started putting his wife before himself. He started turning the TV off and listening to her when she talked to him. He started going by her work and leaving notes. He started helping her with the housework. He started actively loving her. It wasn't that he loved her any more now than before, it was him actively showing it to her that brought about the change. Because of his active love, his wife started changing things as well. Their marriage was changed for the better by a husband who decided he was going to love his wife well! Don't "love" your wife like you "love" candy. Don't be a passive lover! Actively lead, pray, protect, and provide for her!

Don't Break the Unbreakable

A long time ago in a land far, far away, there lived a man whose name was Alex. This may or may not be based on a true story.... But it so is....

My mother was doing some cleaning at her house. She had gotten some new dishes and asked if Tara and I wanted her other set. They were white with blue floral trim around the edges. I remember eating with these plates for the better part of my childhood and teenage years. When I was looking at the plates and thinking about all the meals that had been eaten with them and family time together (yes, I'm sentimental) I turned the plate over and dropped it. (I'm also clumsy). The plate seemed to hang in the balance for a small eternity and then, BAM, right on the hardwood floors. With bated breath, I opened my eyes, and the plate hadn't broken! When I picked up the plate, I noticed something I hadn't seen before. In small print on the bottom of the plate, just below the maker's logo, the word "unbreakable". Now, I'm not sure how you all feel about that word, but all at once the sentimentality wore off and I audibly said: "Challenge accepted, bro!". (Yes, I talk to inanimate objects, don't judge me, man). At that point, I did what any man would do in my position, I started looking for a way to break this plate. I hit it on the kitchen table. WHAM-O! Nothing. Then I'm all like "Well played, Mr. Plate, you're going down, homie!". I bent it across the kitchen counter (or at least I tried). I hit it with a hammer, KABLAM, still in one piece. By this time, as any man would be, I am livid. Blood boiling and red-faced, I lifted the plate over my head, let out my greatest war cry and slammed the plate as hard as I could across my own knee. With a loud pop pieces of the plate (somewhere around 47 million pieces to be exact) went flying in every direction like it had been hit with the Hadouken by Ryu in the last round of *Streetfighter*. The victory was mine at last! It felt good to know I had utterly decimated something considered unbreakable.

Then, my loving mother looked at me with that mom look (you

know the one) and said, "You know where the broom is, clean it up". That stupid plate which had been my great victory over something unbreakable was now spread across my mother's entire house. Literally the whole place, every room somehow had remnants of my mighty destruction. I cleaned for at least 3 days (the space-time continuum had been ripped by my awesome deathblow to the plate... ok, so it was only like an hour, but whatever). For real, I hate sweeping, and it was like everywhere I looked there were more tiny bits of the plate. The victory was less and less sweet the longer it took to clean it up until, eventually, it wasn't a victory at all. Fast forward to a few years later. Mom had to replace her stove and guess what she found under the stove. That's right, pieces of that plate. I thought I had cleaned up my mess, but there it was hiding in a dark corner just waiting to be exposed.

What does a stupid plate have to do with being a godly husband? Everything!

We have been given a great responsibility, gentlemen. We are the drivers. Just like I had the power to break the plate, we've been given the power to lead our families in whatever we think is best. The problem is a lot of men have a misconception of how to use that power. The enemy wants us to believe we are to be more like a dictator than a driver. We are to rule our families with an iron fist when really, we are supposed to lead with a gentle touch. There are a lot of men out there that are harsh to their wives because they think that's what it means to be the "head of the house". I think the verse below proves that this was not what the Lord intended.

> *In the same way, you husbands, live with your wives in an understanding way [with great gentleness and tact, and with an intelligent regard for the marriage relationship], as with someone physically weaker, since she is a woman. Show her honor and respect as a fellow heir of the grace of life, so that your prayers will not be hindered or ineffective.*
>
> 1 PETER 3:7 AMPLIFIED VERSION

This verse tells us two things. How we are supposed to treat our wives and what will happen if we don't obey. Let's start with how we are to treat them. We are told to live with them in an understanding way. We are to be gentle and show them respect. Correct me if I am wrong, but nothing about that verse sounds like a dictator that rules with an iron fist. If you dive deeper into this verse and do a word study, you will find when it says "to be gentle with her like someone physically weaker" you could replace the words "physically weaker" with the words "fragile and valuable." It's not saying they are weak. Tara and my mother are two great examples of what an unbreakable woman looks like, but if mistreated and demeaned they will eventually reach the maximum capacity of what they can take. They can be broken. Peter is saying we are to treat our wives like a crystal vase, or a fine piece of China, something of great sentimental value. We should treat them with care. In other words, we should not try to break the unbreakable. We should instead do everything in our power to preserve it with gentleness and love.

What happens if we decide not to treat our wives with gentleness and love? According to Peter, our prayers will be hindered and ineffective. That is a huge deal, men. The Lord will not answer our prayers if we treat our wives harshly. If the Lord isn't answering our prayers that means our spiritual GPS isn't working. Once the GPS signal is lost the chances of making a wrong turn and getting lost are greater. It gives the enemy entrance to come and lead us down the wrong road. A road that can affect our marriage and our family in a negative way.

Remember, I said earlier, that for years to come we were still finding pieces of that plate? Just like pieces of the plate kept showing up, consequences to our negative actions will keep showing up in our marriage as well if we don't make the decision to go another way. The way we treat our wives will have repercussions for years to come, whether they be good or bad. If we treat them with gentleness and love our wives will have no problem following us. However, if we're domineering, it will be a struggle with negative repercussions.

The trip will always be easier if both the driver and the navigator are working out their position the way the Lord intended.

The Power is Ours

When Tara told me, she was not going to say obey in her vows, I had a decision to make. I could force her to submit to me or I could show her the love Christ showed the church. Tara had an incorrect idea of what submission was, so if I had tried to force her into submission, she would have completely rebelled because I would have validated her incorrect view. By being gentle with her, I, in turn, showed her the true meaning of a godly husband. Was it always easy, no! Did it finally pay off, yes! Once she saw this, she had no problem jumping in the passenger seat and following me. Just like on our vacations, she trusts that I will lead her where we are supposed to go.

We have the power to break the unbreakable, but do you really want to pick up the pieces for years to come? I sure don't. Making the choice to preserve something valuable by loving and leading well is a far greater victory than cleaning up the mess after the destruction has happened. The power to love and lead our families has been given to us by the Father! It's the way we choose to love and lead that will determine where we will end up. It's the way we use this power that will determine if we have a beautiful adventure with our spouse or end up stranded on the side of the road. I choose a beautiful adventure!

PART 2

Maintain the Necessities

CHAPTER 4

THE TIRES (FORGIVENESS)

"A happy marriage is a union of two good forgivers"
~ Ruth Bell Graham

With our bags packed and our relationship roles defined, let's dive into a subject that is crucial for a happy marriage. Regardless of all the prep work, our adventure can be doomed from the beginning if this one thing isn't practiced early and often... forgiveness. With this book, I'm likening marriage to an adventure we get to go on, with the one we love. I wanted to link the topics of every chapter to something physical that would help us on an actual adventure. When I was thinking about forgiveness tires instantly came to mind. In marriage, forgiveness is essential just like good tires and maintenance on those tires are essential for a successful road trip. If we don't learn to forgive quickly and often, all the other things we're going to talk about in this book won't be as effective. Holding on to unforgiveness toward your spouse is like having a leaky tire on your car. If it's not addressed it will get you a little further down the road; however, the result of the leak will become greater and greater and eventually you'll be on the side of the road with a flat tire unable to continue on your journey until it's fixed.

We are imperfect people. We all make mistakes, some intentionally some accidentally. Forgiveness is something we all need to extend and receive pretty much daily. When you first meet the one, you're going to marry, things are perfect. They're perfect. You're perfect. Everything is perfect. During that period forgiveness seems unnecessary, doesn't it? Why would we ever need forgiveness? Everything is perfect! As time goes on and you get married you start to realize all the things that were perfect, to begin with, aren't actually perfect. Things get forgotten, hurtful words get spoken, and feelings get hurt. I would say the majority of the time hurting each other isn't what was intended, but again, we're two imperfect people doing life together-it happens. Regardless of the what, when, where, and how behind the conflict forgiveness is necessary if any relationship is going to thrive and grow! In this chapter, we are going to address some reasons why we may be allowing the slow leak of unforgiveness to happen in our marriages, ways to patch the leak, and ways to keep the leaks from happening in the first place. This chapter is not a chapter you will visit once. This will be a topic you will have to revisit repeatedly for the duration of your marriage adventure. In fact, you might as well go ahead and invest in a timeshare with forgiveness because you will be using it often.

Leaks, Flats, and Blowouts

In my very limited amount of tire knowledge, I can think of three ways we have problems with the air in our tires. Sometimes the leak is very small and takes a long time to cause any inconvenience on our part. Sometimes the leak happens quickly, and you can feel a difference in how your car is riding because the tire is losing air rapidly. Then there is the blowout that can cause a wreck if one doesn't know how to handle the car. All three of these problems need a solution because they all lead to the same end. However, the person with the slow leak may not go and fix their tire as quickly as the person that has the blowout. Maybe they don't know the leak is there, or maybe they do but it isn't affecting their life right now, so they choose not to deal with it. Choosing not to deal with the problem will lead to bigger problems with a car, and the same is true of a relationship. Problems left unpatched in a marriage will eventually lead to blowouts.

Let's look at three ways conflict happens in our marriages. There are times where the conflict is not very noticeable. You're aware it's there, but it isn't directly affecting your daily life, so you choose not to deal with it. These are the little hurts and hang-ups. These are hurtful words or tones. These are the accidental mistakes that happen unintentionally, but they still sting. They seem so insignificant we choose not to address them. The issue is these little moments tend to add up when there is no closure or resolution. Then there are times when the conflict is noticeable. It affects you at that moment because it's adding some bumps to your marriage. These situations are a little bigger. Maybe some of these are intentional. Two imperfect people living in small spaces tend to get underneath each other's skin. These are the times when things happen, and words are said which leave a mark. Perhaps deep down we know they didn't mean to hurt us, but they did, and we don't see how it can be undone. Then there are the all-out blowouts. These are the big ones. No one enjoys these because they bring you to a standstill. Trust may have been broken. Blowouts seem unforgivable and definitely unrepairable. These are the moments the enemy likes to swoop in and tell you a completely new tire is needed. Just discard this messed up one.

Forgiveness and closure are critical in all three of the situations. If we can learn to forgive and move on when we have a leak, we can avoid the blow out altogether. If we can learn to extend forgiveness, a blowout can be repaired. No problem, big or small, is just going to fix itself. A problem left unfixed regardless of the size will only become a bigger problem. However, any problem can be fixed when two people forgive each other and ask God to help them to fix whatever is broken. It takes communicating and forgiveness in a marriage to make the ride smooth. It takes those hard conversations which no one enjoys for us to get to the closure needed to move on. Don't avoid the small pothole and run into a ditch because of unforgiveness, and unresolved conflict. If you have already hit the ditch don't believe the lie that the ditch is the end of your adventure either. If you're willing to walk this forgiveness thing out, God is faithful to help you fix whatever needs fixing. God is the Master Mechanic.

Lies We Believe About Forgiveness

I will be the first to make a confession that I'm sure is running through your mind right now. Forgiveness is hard! At this moment, you may have a particular situation or person in your brain, and you may be thinking of a hundred different reasons why forgiveness isn't an option for you. I get it, and yes, forgiveness is very hard to walk out sometimes. I believe one reason it's hard is because we have the wrong idea of what forgiveness actually is. When I had the wrong definition of "submit" I couldn't carry out my role properly and I think the same thing is happening in marriages every day with forgiveness. We have an enemy that likes to distort the true meaning of things, so we have problems with them. He has done a great job distorting the definition of forgiveness. Let's look at some lies the enemy has led us to believe as to why we can't forgive and let's see how this might affect our marriage and our lives in general.

"I will forgive them when I feel like forgiving them."

I'm just going to be blunt for a second. When do we ever "feel" like forgiving someone? Seriously, when do we ever "feel" like doing anything uncomfortable, challenging, or that forces us to acknowledge our own shortcomings? How about never! We can't go with our feelings on this one. We must make a choice to forgive. You must make up your mind that you're going to forgive them and then you must act in accordance with that decision. You may still feel the anger or hurt, and it may take some time for those feelings to diminish depending on what exactly happened. However, it's in those moments of hurt that we have a decision to make. Forgiveness isn't always a one and done thing. In fact, in most cases, we will have to make the choice to forgive multiple times before our feelings line up with our decision. A friend of mine once said, "choices lead, feelings follow." This statement is so true, but we all want it to be the other way around. We want to wait and feel like it. There are a lot of people out there reaping the consequences of unforgiveness simply because they're waiting to have the feeling of forgiveness. It's time to stop waiting. It's time to make the choice today to forgive. It's time to make the choice and then make the choice again and again until your feelings line up with the decision you have made.

- Lie- Forgiveness is a feeling!
- Truth- Forgiveness is a choice!

"I will forgive them when they ask me too."

Ideally, this one makes sense. As soon as the other person comes up and ask for forgiveness (preferably on their knees, groveling, with some kind of homemade baked good) I will be more than happy to forgive them. This excuse takes the spotlight off us and puts it on them. The issue is in most cases people aren't going to come and ask for forgiveness. They may genuinely want too but they, like us, have an enemy lying to them telling them we would never forgive them, or they are waiting on their feelings to line up too. (Ahem, we all have the same enemy telling us lies.) It may be that they are just flat out not sorry. Then, there are the times, they really have no idea they have hurt you at all, so they don't know to ask for forgiveness or to explain the misunderstanding. This one can occur in marriages often. Your spouse may have done something to hurt your feelings but genuinely not know they have done so. Now you are upset and waiting for them to ask for forgiveness while they have no idea a hurt has occurred. Sometimes it takes going to the other person yourself to get the closure you need. The person holding on to the unforgiveness in these situations is always the one who is suffering not the person that's oblivious. Regardless of your situation, forgiveness is more about what you need than what they need. We need to extend forgiveness as much as we need to receive it. Harboring those hurt feelings and not letting something go is far more harmful to us than it is for them.

- Lie- Forgive is for the other person!
- Truth- Forgiveness is for us!

"I can't forgive that."

This is one of the biggest lies of the enemy. Now before I go on with this, I want to address the fact that there are some people who have genuinely been through some horrendous events. You've been hurt in a way that is so deep that healing and forgiveness may seem completely impossible. I don't want to imply that this kind of forgiveness is easy or that you should just "get over" what happened. I understand some hurts take time. I also understand that some of the deepest hurts happen between a husband and a wife. What I am trying to say is, thinking that you "can't" forgive is a lie from the enemy. He likes to plant this little gem into our hearts because he knows as I stated in the previous section that we are the ones that suffer from unforgiveness.

This kind of forgiveness is a true lifetime process. It may take years to completely heal and be able to truly say that you have forgiven them. Here is the wonderful news, the Lord honors steps of obedience and He is the God of restoration. If you will just make those small daily decisions to forgive, the Lord will come alongside you and help you. He doesn't expect you to "get over it" in a moment and then pretend like it never happened. In fact, quite the opposite is true. Don't be afraid to walk through this process, you are not alone. Don't be discouraged that it's taking too long. The Lord is patient and loves when His children are walking in obedience especially when it is hard. The Lord can do amazing things when we make the choice to forgive.

- Lie- I can't forgive that!
- Truth- With God's help I can forgive anything!

These are just a few examples of the lies that the enemy uses to try and keep us from forgiving, and he loves to use these lies in our marriage. He knows a couple walking in unity is a focus to be reckoned with, so he tries everything to cause division. I pray this chapter exposes him for the liar he is. You can forgive your spouse! It may take time and a lot of grace from the Lord, but forgiveness and restoration are always possible when you take a step of obedience combined with the Lord's help. Don't let the lies of the enemy continue to cause tire problems on your marriage adventure.

Patching the Tires

Now we know we have an enemy that loves to lie to us and tell us we "cannot" or "should not" forgive. Now that we know some of the lies the enemy uses to keep us from forgiving, let's talk about some ways to forgive. Some of you have been through some incredibly bad situations. Some things are hard to forgive but remember, forgiveness is for us not for them. We need to forgive them more than they need our forgiveness. This is never truer than in marriage. You can't have a happy marriage if one or both of you are holding on to some wrong or hurt feelings. Forgiveness and the acceptance of forgiveness must be actively pursued to make a marriage work. Let's talk about a few daily decisions you can make regarding your spouse that can help you walk in forgiveness every day.

• Pray for Them

We're going to talk about this one a lot throughout this entire book. Prayer is so vitally important in every aspect of marriage and just life in general. Prayer is one of the greatest weapons and privileges we've been given by our Father. So how can prayer help us with forgiveness?

First, it helps us remember how much we have been forgiven. I don't know about you, but I constantly mess up and have to ask the Father to forgive me and help me do better. Frankly, this happens on a daily basis. Here is the beautiful part, He always forgives and helps me. By praying for my spouse, it helps me remember the grace that has so lavishly been poured unto me so I can then, in turn, extend it to Alex. Praying helps me remember all the chances the Father has given me and how He never gave up on me. With this in mind, it makes it easier for me to forgive Alex as many times as needed.

Secondly, prayer not only changes the situation, it changes us. Prayer has the power to transform and restore any situation we may find ourselves in by changing the way we view the situation. I once heard that prayer is like a tower. If we pray, we can see further and understand more about our surroundings and what is happening so we can make wise decisions. It makes us more alert and perceptive. Regarding marriage, it gives us some insight into the other person. It changes our perspective as it were. When I pray for Alex it reminds me, he is a child of God, just like I am. He wants to do what is right, just like I do. It reminds me, he is not my enemy, we are a team working toward the same goal. Prayer allows me to pause and really consider the intentions behind Alex's words and actions instead of just reacting based on what I think his intentions are. Prayer gives us insight we don't have on our own and with that insight, we can make the decision to respond to our spouse with grace instead of reacting in anger.

Now, how does prayer help when your spouse has done something very hurtful and very intentional? First, praying for them heals us because we get to go to God and be real. We get to go to God and tell Him how badly it hurt us. We get to go to Him and be raw. When we pray to God, we don't have to hold anything back because He is a big God that can handle our big feelings. But, the wild thing about praying boldly and openly to God is He takes that hurt and He begins to heal it. When we take those feelings to the only One that can mend them, we get to walk away restored and transformed. Will it be a process? Absolutely! But God is a faithful God who always fixes our broken pieces if we'll just bring them to Him. He will patch our leaky tires so we can continue our adventure.

Lastly, we serve a God that does not leave anyone out. He loves our spouses just as much as He loves us. He loves the one that hurt as much as He loves the one hurting. When we pray for our spouses in those moments of deep hurt, we are handing them over to God so He can do some restorative work on them as well. Our prayers are powerful, friends, and by praying in those moments, when you probably really don't feel like praying, you are inviting God to come in and God never leaves a place the way He finds it. He can turn a total blow out into a beautiful thing. When we give our spouses over to God and earnestly pray, the Lord will do a work in them. Again, it may be a process. You may have to pray for them for a while before you see any real change but be patient and let God do what only God can do.

- Show them Kindness

After you have prayed for them, now it's time to show them kindness. If you want restoration in your marriage you may have to be the first person to start the process. If you want your marriage to last you may have to step up and be the bigger person. Don't wait for them to make the first move. Don't give them a cold shoulder. Don't pray for them and then treat them as if you will never forgive them. That kind of behavior will get you nowhere and it shows you have some issues that may need to be addressed as well. Maybe it's time to pray and then act? Maybe it's time to be the man or woman God has called you to be? Here's the thing, most of the time, the things we get our feelings hurt over are not big deals. Really think about that, is my situation genuinely a big deal? If so, I suggest getting counseling or a pastor to mentor you and help you through the process, but if it isn't, just be the bigger person and move on. Sometimes you have to pick your battles. Sometimes you have to ask yourself if it is really worth fighting about.

In my opinion being angry and arguing with Alex is such a waste of the time we've been given. When I find myself angry, aggravated, or hurt I have gotten in the habit of asking myself, "Is it worth the time?" Most of the time, it isn't so I go on with my life. The times it is Alex and I deal with it (communication, compromise, or forgiveness) and move on. Most of the time those conversations aren't fun, but my goodness the closure that comes at the end of them is so good. Once we have found closure and decided to "move on" we both act like it. We don't bring it back up and we don't give each other the silent treatment. We may still feel the hurt or angry (those feelings don't go away instantly) and we may have to go do something alone to regain ourselves, but when we come back together, we treat each other in a way that shows forgiveness has happened. I encourage you today, please don't waste the time you have been given. Deal with what needs to be dealt with then go back to enjoying each other.

Routine and Planned Maintenance

As I was preparing to write this chapter, I kept thinking about forgiveness being our tires for this journey. Our tires keep us safe and moving down the road and if we're quick to forgive and extend forgiveness our marriages will continue smoothly on its adventure. So, I started googling some things about tires because basically, all I knew was "the wheels on the bus go round and round". I know very little about cars and tires. I let Alex handle all that madness. I looked up what tires did and why they were important. I found out, tires do way more than just go "round and round". According to google, this is the purpose and function of a tire~ *While **tires** do tend to get overlooked, they are arguably the most **important component** on your vehicle. ... The main functions of a vehicle's **tires** include supporting the vehicle load, transmitting traction and braking forces to the road surface, absorbing road shocks, and changing and maintaining the direction of travel.*

After googling this, and then asking Alex what it meant, I found out tires help support the load, they adhere to the road which makes it possible for us to take off, stop, and stay on the road altogether, and they take on the majority of the shock from the roads so we will be as comfortable as possible. So, let's swing this to forgiveness. In marriage when we forgive one another it takes the load off the other person and our relationship, it helps us to move forward after a disagreement, it keeps us on course, and it makes our adventure smoother and more comfortable.

I also learned something else about tires. They must have maintenance to continue to do the job they were created to do. I knew the tires needed maintenance to perform well, but I didn't know there are two kinds of maintenance needed to maintain the quality and effectiveness of your tires. There is routine maintenance and planned maintenance. According to google -*Routine maintenance also known as preventive, preventative, or cyclical maintenance, is an essential part of the ongoing care and upkeep of any car. Planned preventive maintenance, more commonly referred to as simply planned maintenance or scheduled maintenance, is any variety of scheduled maintenance to an object or item of equipment.* We all know if we take the time to perform maintenance on our cars they run better. I think we should start taking the time to perform the same kind of maintenance in our marriage.

Performing this maintenance will help us to forgive and receive forgiveness which will improve our marriages. So, what does this maintenance look like?

Routine - Preventative Maintenance

- Love Deposits

If we want our tires to stay in good shape, we must do routine maintenance. We must take the car to the shop and have the pressure and tire tread checked. If we are intentional about this, a problem can be spotted early and taken care of cheaper and easier than if we didn't do preventative maintenance. We have talked about how a simple problem, if left unfixed on a tire, can turn into a huge blowout. Because this is also true with marriage, we need routine maintenance as well. We need to do preventative work, so a blowout doesn't happen further down the road. We do this by daily showing our spouse grace and love. When Alex and I were engaged a couple in our lives introduced us to something they called "Love Deposits". Think about the actual tires on your car. They need air in them to operate at their full capacity. A tire that is low on air makes for a rough ride. However, if we're consistent on gauging the air and then depositing more when it's needed, we will experience a smooth ride. The same principle works in our marriage. We need to constantly gauge how we are treating our spouse and make deposits every day. We can make these deposits a million different ways- speaking their love language, giving them our full attention, etc. You make a deposit with every act of goodness and kindness you give.

We can cause a leak in our relationship in a million different ways also- unkind words, disagreements, etc. Just like with our tires, if you have made deposits into your spouse the leaks will not have as great of a negative effect. Forgiveness can usually be extended freely because you have stored up a lot of love deposits. However, if you haven't made enough love deposits then the leaks will not be as easy to forgive and move on. Whether it is a leaky tire, or a problem in your marriage, if you take the time to do preventative work the problem will not be as expensive or as difficult to fix. Making love deposit is a way of performing routine maintenance on your marriage. You are doing the work in advance to guarantee a successful trip. Will there be an unexpected leak? Yes. But you will be able to spot them early and repair them quickly.

Planned Maintenance-Scheduled Maintenance

- What do I know to be true?

Like I said earlier, leaks will happen. We are two imperfect people doing life together. No matter how hard you try, there will be times when you disagree or say things that are hurtful. What do you do after the leak has been discovered? When it comes to your tires, you typically go to a shop and have a professional mechanic fix it or, if you are super handy, you go buy the supplies and fix it yourself. That decision usually depends on the severity of the leak. If the leak is bad enough you may need to get professional help. There is no shame in going to the shop and having a professional help you. The same is true for your marriage. Going to a counselor or a pastor is not a shameful thing. In fact, if the problem can't be solved alone, it's a wise thing. Investing in your marriage in the efforts to correct it and grow it is worth it. Don't wait, schedule an appointment to get the maintenance that is needed. My one encouragement here is to not seek out help from anyone that will stand still long enough for you to tell them the story. Find that one pastor, counselor, or godly mentor that can be trusted and will pray with and for you. We need to seek professional help, not just any help. It will do you no good if the person trying to help you has no clue what they are doing. You wouldn't take your car to a random person for help, right? You would take it to a mechanic. So, why take your marriage issues to a random person? Find someone that is godly and wise to ask for help.

Now, if you can handle it on your own, great! One-way Alex and I handle scheduled maintenance if by asking ourselves one simple question. 'What do I know to be true?" Let me show you what this looks like, because we both do this in different ways. Let's say Alex and I are having a problem that has led to hurt feelings and my feelings are telling me lies about Alex. Maybe I think, "Alex doesn't care about me." Instead of meditating on that lie, I ask myself that question and then I answer it. I remember all the times Alex has shown me he genuinely cares about me. I then state the truth to overpower the lie. "I know Alex cares about me because he does__". Then I fill in the blank with examples of Alex showing me he cares. Alex does this totally different than I do. When he is upset with me, and a lie pops in his head about me, he thinks about 1 Corinthians 13:4-8. He reads those verses on love, then he puts my name in them everywhere the word love is used. Tara is patient. Tara is kind. In both cases, we are taking the lie and replacing it with the truth. We are looking at the past deposits that have been made and it makes us realize the deposits outweigh whatever is causing the leak. By using this one simple question, Alex and I have been able to see the problem for what it is instead of what the enemy wants us to believe. We see it's fixable, we fix it, and move on.

A Leak and a Lie

When we have a leak, the enemy wants us to believe, the entire tire is ruined and needs to be thrown away. That is why so many marriages end in divorce. We focus on the problem and not the solution. We buy into the lie that says the problem is huge and it's not worth the maintenance. We buy into the lie that says we bought the wrong tire, to begin with, and another tire would never leak. It hurts my heart to think about all the couples that have given up all because of a leak and a lie. Now, you may be thinking, my marriage doesn't have a leak, we have experienced a full-on blowout. How is that fixable? By human ability, your situation may seem utterly impossible to fix, but we serve a God that can heal the sick, raise the dead, and restore the broken. It doesn't matter how bad your blow out is, if you ask God to come and help you fix it, He will. Below are a few Bible verses I hope will encourage you that God can fix the blowouts in our marriages.

> *And He who sits on the throne said, "Behold, I am making all things new." Also, He said, "Write, for these words are faithful and true [they are accurate, incorruptible, and trustworthy]."*
> *REVELATIONS 21:5 AMPLIFIED VERSION*

> *But Jesus looked at them and said, "With people [as far as it depends on them] it is impossible, but with God all things are possible."*
> *MATTHEW 19:26 AMPLIFIED BIBLE*

Take these verses and find more that speaks to your situation. Memorize them, meditate on them, put them where you can see them every day, and speak them out loud. Let God's promises penetrate your heart until you fully believe He will do what He says He will do. Then, you go do your part, which is to forgive and receive forgiveness. Let today be the day you decide to perform the maintenance your marriage needs. Let today be the day you look at the problem, see it is fixable, and fix it. Let today be the day you let forgiveness change your marriage.

I want to leave you with this final verse on forgiveness.

> *For if you forgive others their trespasses [their reckless and willful sins], your heavenly Father will also forgive you. But if*

you do not forgive others [nurturing your hurt and anger with the result that it interferes with your relationship with God], then your Father will not forgive your trespasses.

Matthew 6:14-15 Amplified Version

Jesus makes it very plain in these two verses. If we forgive, we will be forgiven, but if we don't, the Lord will not forgive us. That's a scary truth we need to really take to heart. Unforgiveness is not worth the consequences, friends! It's not a suggestion, but a command from our God that loves us with an indescribable love. He knows what is best for us. The Lord can do more than we could ever imagine if we will just give our hurts to Him. Be willing and obedient and watch the Lord do what only He can. He is the Master Mechanic! Take your leaks and blowouts to Him! If we will forgive, He can change our lives and our marriages!

CHAPTER 5

THE GEARS (PASSIONATE PURSUIT)

"I would rather die of passion than of boredom."
~Vincent Van Gogh

I chased a bear into the woods...
Now, when I say I chased a bear, I mean that in the most literal sense. I loudly and passionately chased a bear in the mountains of Tennessee. Let me tell you how I got to this moment.

Alex and I have been married for 7 years. Very early in our marriage, Alex found out I wanted to see a bear in it's natural habitat. He made it his personal mission for me to see one. He has taken me to Gatlinburg, Tennessee, on multiple occasions, with no bear sightings. When we went to Colorado last year he googled and found the campsite with the highest bear sightings and we camped there for two days- no bears. When we went to Maine, we kept our eyes open for a possible bear- nothing. When I say that Alex has driven me all over this beautiful country for years to see a bear, it's the honest truth. In October of 2018, we decided to go to Gatlinburg with some friends on a vacation. I was hoping maybe on this trip we would be successful, and I would see one. I had often wondered what that moment would look like when I actually saw this creature. Let me take a few moments and paint the picture for you.

We were driving back to our cabin and the sun was very bright. Alex and Andy were in the front seat and Penny and I were in the back. We were all talking when Alex turned the corner and the sun blinded him. I looked up and crossing the street was a black bear. My brain processed what it was, but I couldn't get the word "bear" out of my mouth, so I start screaming like a crazy person. Andy saw it and yelled, "Bear!". Keep in mind, Alex is still blinded, and Penny has no idea why everyone is screaming. Andy starts yelling at him to go, I am frantically trying to open my car door (yes, the car is moving) but I couldn't get it to open. We pull up to where it had crossed, and Andy lets me out of the car. We both go running down the street along the tree line after this bear! I am still making random squealing noise because words still haven't come yet. Andy sees it in the woods points it out to me and I dropped to my knees with arms extended as I violently scream, "COME BACK BEAR!" At this point, the bear takes off never to be seen again!

In my mind, my first encounter was going to be a peaceful quiet moment. I had dreamed about it many times, and every time it was quiet and serene. However, when it came, it was wild, loud, and beautifully chaotic. Although my first encounter didn't go as I had imagined, it was an experience I will never forget for many reasons. One, I had seen a bear in it's natural habitat, something I had wanted for several years, and two, the Lord used this experience to teach me a lesson. The next morning, when Jesus and I were spending time together, I was still thinking about that moment and I was thanking Him that I had finally seen a bear. He took me off guard when He asked me this question.

"What if you chased after Me like you chased that bear?"

Can we just take a moment to let that question sink in? I have been all over the country in search of this one thing. I have been passionately looking and waiting for the moment I would see this bear. What if I search for Jesus in this passionate way? What if I was that intentional? What if I was that passionate? What if I was that relentless in my pursuit of Him? What if I was that loud and wild about Him? What would my relationship be like if my pursuit of Him looked like my pursuit of that bear? The Lord didn't stop there. Then He branched off the question concerning Alex.

"What would your marriage look like if you pursued Alex with that much passion?"

It has been over a year since I had my encounter with the bear and my moment with the Lord, but I'm still letting those two questions sink into my soul. What would my life look like if I pursued the Lord and Alex with that much intensity? What would other marriages look like if both spouses pursued the Lord and each other with that much intensity? I believe we would see this world change in unimaginable ways. I believe we would see marriages change in unimaginable ways. Since October I have been trying to walk out this passionate pursuit in my own life. My moment with the Lord has spurred me on to turn that passionate pursuit inside of me outward and upward-outward to my husband and upward toward Jesus. I don't want to be passive about them and passionate about a bear. God has used this moment in my life to encourage me to use something that was inside of me all along- wild and active passion. In this chapter, we are going to talk about ways to pursue God and our spouses in the correct way, and ways to "shift our gears" so we are pursuing them actively and deliberately. You will discover being passionate about your spouse isn't hard, in fact, it may be way easier than you ever thought possible. Let's get started.

Pursue God, Pursue Your Spouse

And he replied, "You shall love the Lord your God with all your heart, and with all your soul, and with all your strength, and with all your mind; and your neighbor as yourself.

Luke 10:27 Amplified Version

Let's take the trip back in time that I ask the ladies to take in chapter two. Did anyone have a problem passionately pursuing their future spouse in the dating period or in the engagement period? I sure didn't! I always wanted to talk to and spend time Alex. He was my number one priority. I put him above everything and everyone else including God for a time. Although we do need to put our spouses in a position of honor, I want to start this chapter by saying we must put them in the correct position of honor. I will be the first to say that when Alex and I were dating I didn't have my priorities in order at all. We must put God first and our spouses second. We need to pursue God with our whole hearts before we can pursue our spouses correctly. If we put our spouse in the place of God, disappointment and heartache will be the only things in our future. Why? Because our spouses are not equipped to supply everything for us and if we put that responsibility on them, they will not add up. It took me some time to get things in the right order. I bet when you read the title of this chapter you did not think that we would start off by talking about our passion towards God; however, if we don't get this one thing in the correct order other things in our lives will not fall into place either.

The above verse from Luke is very clear. We are to love God and then love people. We are to love God totally with everything in us. Our relationship with the Lord should be of the highest importance to us. It should be regarded as precious. It should be a part of our daily lives. What would your relationship with your spouse look like if you only spent one hour a week with them? We understand if we did that with our spouses, we wouldn't have a relationship at all! Yet we do this with God and expect everything in our lives to fall into place. Now, before you think I'm throwing stones, remember, I admitted earlier I was there. When Alex and I met, I was saved, I loved the Lord, and I went to church, but He was not a part of my daily life. I didn't pray very consistently, and I didn't set aside any time for Him daily. I read my Bible, but I wasn't really taking anything away from what I was reading. It was more of a duty than a time to grow. It wasn't until a few years ago, I got very intentional about my time with the Lord. Now, He is a part of my everyday life and because of that, I have changed in so many ways. So, before we start talking about passionately pursuing our spouses, I encourage you to passionately pursue the Lord. Give Him space in your everyday life. Pray to Him daily. Be intentional about it. It doesn't have to look like anyone else's time. You can take 5 minutes, or 5 hours, just take the time to pursue that relationship first and He will come in and do the work only He can do. It will not only benefit you, but all your relationships as well.

Get Your Butt in Gear

Passion is a strong and barely controllable emotion

Ever since the bear moment, I have given a lot of thought to what a passionate pursuit looks like and how I can translate that to my relationships. I decided that I wanted to give the Lord and Alex my all. To do that I had to do a little studying into what a passionate pursuit looked like, I mean let's face it, I can't chase my husband into the woods every day screaming for him to come back. Through everything, I kept seeing the words active and passive. There is the active passionate pursuit of someone or something and then there is the passive pursuit. According to dictionary.com~ *Active means involving physical effort and action whereas Passive means accepting what happens without active response or resistance.*

If I was going to pursue Alex correctly, I would have to put forth

77

some effort and action. My mind instantly went to the gears in a car. You can turn your car on all day, but if you don't put it in the right gear it will just sit in one place and idle. Yes, it's on. Yes, it can move, go fast, and take you on the adventure of a lifetime, but if it's not in the correct gear it won't be able to do any of the things it is capable of. It won't be able to do the very things it was created to do! And that isn't even the worst part. If we just let a car idle, eventually it will run out of gas, die, and movement will not be possible at all. This is the picture that comes to mind when I think of a passionless marriage, an idle car slowly going dead. A relationship that is capable of so much more, so much passion, fun, and adventure yet it's just idling in one place. I don't want this for my marriage, but if I choose to be passive, it will happen and the same goes for everyone else.

When I was a child my mama used to say something to me when she needed me to hurry up. She would look at me and affectionately say, "Tara, get your butt in gear, let's go!" As a kid, this meant, "Ok, time to stop messing around. She is getting serious". As an adult, wanting a passionate marriage, it means the exact same thing! If we want a passionate marriage, we need to "get our butts in gear" and actively pursue our spouses every day! We need to get serious about it and make sure we are in the right gear. So how do we do that? I knew ways Alex and I pursued each other, but I wanted to learn about what other couples were doing to keep passion alive in their marriages. So, I started asking other couples I knew what a passionate pursuit of their spouses looked like to them. Here are a few of the examples they gave me on how they shift gears in order to pursue their spouses.

~One lady said-For me, passion and honor go hand in hand. I feel more passionate about my husband when he honors me in a loving way. It is usually in the small things like- opening a car door, always let me speaks first and really listening to what I have to say, acknowledging my presence when we are in a crowd or when I walk into

the room, or watching a show I want to watch. A big one for me is I know he does not speak negatively about me to other people. He treats me like God's daughter and because of that, I feel passionate towards him. Because of that, I want to be just as passionate about him because it is a two-way street. Her husband resonated her same thought with-You put her first-always. It could be as simple as just doing something, so she doesn't have too. Regardless of how you are feeling you should always have a servant's heart toward her.

~One couple told me they feel the passion in their marriage when they minister together. They feel united when they get to speak life into people that have lost their hope. Knowing that they are doing what they were created to do together ignites passion.

~One lady told me she loves the date nights that she and her husband share alone. She loves to have his undivided attention and spending that time together is passionate for her. Her husband's response was unique to me. He said he does not feel like he is very passionate, so he is very intentional about speaking her love language. He knows when he does acts of service for her she feels love so to make up for what he sees as a weakness he speaks her language fluently.

As I was talking to these couples, I realized each one of them made the daily the deliberate. They were staying in the right gear by being intentional about words and deeds when it came to their spouses. They put forth the effort every day to do things just for their spouses. Through all their advice, I saw one of the main ways I could pursue Alex was putting his needs above my own. I needed to put him first in order to pursue him well. Let's talk about some ways we can shift our gears and put our spouse before ourselves.

Shifting Gears

Put Your Spouse Before Yourself

We have already talked about putting God first. So, you know that I'm not talking about putting your spouse in front of God, what I am talking about is putting your spouse in front of yourself and all the other people in your life. This doesn't mean neglect yourself or the other relationships, it just means we should care about our spouse's needs, feelings, and opinions first and foremost. They shouldn't be the last person we consider; they should be the first! Alex and I put each other first by doing simple things on a regular basis. As I share some of the ways we put each other first, you may think they are silly. Maybe so, but we do them with the sole intent of showing the other person we value them.

- First Gear- Consider their Opinion

Let's start with the one that might shock you, our hair and our clothes! Hair is very important to us or at least it is very important to me. Before Alex goes to get his hair cut, we talk about what he is going to do. Honestly, Alex could care less about his own hair, but he knows I love it, so he includes me in the decisions about it and I do the same with mine. Every time Alex includes me in this decision, it makes me feel like he values my opinion and wants to make me happy. I do the same with him with my clothes. He has voiced his opinion that there are certain fashion trends he just doesn't like, so I try to stay away from those, and buy certain outfits because I know he would like them. He is the person I want to impress by the way I look, so I intentionally try to do things based on that. I wasn't super intentional about my clothes and Alex's opinion on them until I was watching an Instagram story one night. There is a certain lady that leads a ministry that I follow. Around 9:30 she posted a video of her at home. She had been busy all day and she was in her pajamas waiting for her husband to get home. About twenty minutes later she posted another video, fully dressed, and putting on high heels. She explained she had just realized she hadn't seen her husband all day and she wanted to surprise him by looking her best when he arrived home. She went on to say his opinion of how she looked was the most important to her so that's why she was getting dressed up. This really made me think. Did she have to do this? Of course not! If she had been in her pajamas when he got home, he would have completely understood. It was almost 10 o'clock. But, by doing this she was putting him first. It paid off for her too. When he got home, and saw how pretty she looked, he ended up taking her on a late-night date. Now, I want to make this very plain, just like that couple, Alex and I don't do this because we have too. Alex could cut his hair any way he likes, and I could wear any clothes I want. We don't force each other to do this. We do this because our main goal is to put the other one first by considering their opinion.

As I was writing this, I asked Alex what were some ways he felt we put each other first by considering each other's opinion. One of his answers actually shocked me. It happened the night before. When I was taking some chicken out of the freezer for supper, I grab a piece of chicken for me and steak for him. I didn't give it much thought; I just know he isn't a big fan of chicken and he would enjoy steak more. Alex said that showed I was thinking of him and that one act spoke love to him because it showed I was taking his opinion into account. I realized I am spending a lot of time talking about simple things like hair, clothes, and food, but this should encourage you! Why? Because pursuing your spouse isn't hard. Shifting gear doesn't have to be a long drawn out process or a big elaborate event. You can make the daily, the deliberate! You can pursue your spouse every day by just thinking about their wants, needs, and opinions. By just asking yourself, "What would they like?", you are shifting gears and pursuing them in an active way. By following through and doing the things they like you are showing them in small everyday moments they are important to you and you care about them.

- Second Gear- Honor Them

Honor- *high respect; great esteem.*

We talked a little bit about honor in chapter two when I was talking to the wives. Wives honor their husbands by submitting to them as the Lord asked us too. We talked about several ways we could submit to our husbands. Those steps can be used by both people to pursue their spouses by honoring them. However, there are other ways to honor your spouse as well.

One of the couples I talked to mentioned she felt honored when her husband acknowledged her presence. When she walks up to him when he is talking to someone else or she enters the room when he is watching tv, just the fact that he stops for a moment and acknowledges her, makes her feel honored. It may be as simple as a quick smile or taking her by the hand, but that small gesture speaks volumes to her. By taking those few seconds to acknowledge her, he is letting her know that regardless of what is going on, her presence matters to him. What a simple yet beautiful way of shifting gears! Another way we can honor our spouses is by simply helping them. The husband of the lady I mentioned above said that was one of the ways he honors her. He does things just so she doesn't have too. Simply put, if you know they have things to do, see if you can take something off their plate. I can attest to this one. I typically have about fifteen irons in the fire, so when Alex does something for me, and I don't have to it, it's a big deal. It frees me up to finish what I am working on, without becoming overwhelmed, or it frees me up to spend that extra time with him, which is always great.

A big way we can put our spouses in a place of honor is by letting them be our first point of contact. Who do you go to when something bad or good happens? Who's the first person you run to with any kind of news? What's the first number you dial when you need help? Whose opinion or advice do you take most of the time? This may seem like an obvious answer but really think about it. You and your spouse are a team. Alex and I like to say it's us against the world. Your spouse should be the person you go to first. Their number should be the first you dial when there is news. Their opinion or advice should be the first you consider. There are times outside influences are needed. We have talked about the importance of mentors, but we shouldn't go to them before we have gone to our spouse first. Alex and I have had issues come up or decisions we needed to make that we needed our mentors to help us with; however, we didn't go to them until after we had talked to each other and then agreed we needed outside help. It's easy to put other people or even social media platforms ahead of our spouse if we aren't careful. This is something we must be intentional about. It doesn't always have to be bad or big things either. Who do you go to first when something great happens? Do you call a friend, put it on social media, or tell your spouse? Again, a simple decision of telling them first puts them in that place of honor.

These are just a few simple ways to shift your gears and pursue your spouse passionately by daily putting your spouse first and honoring them. I hope you see, by the examples I used, it doesn't have to be hard. We are always hearing how hard marriage is and there are times that marriage is very hard. But everything doesn't have to be hard. We can make super simple decisions every day that helps to make marriage easier. If you're intentional about making those simple decisions to pursue your spouse consistently you will see a big change in your marriage. Now let's talk about how to pursue our spouses by shifting into high gear-sex!

High Gear

The "S" Word

Several years ago, Alex and I were at a family gathering. One of our cousins told us a story about their son who was very young at the time. Something happened and the son was upset with his parents. In the midst of his frustration, he looked at his parents and said, "If y' all don't stop it, I'm going to use the "S" word." His parents, assuming he was going to say a word he shouldn't say, asked him what the "s" word was. In a very serious tone he said, "Sex, I don't know what it is, but I have heard it's awful."

Alex and I bring that story up often and we still think it's one of the funniest things we have ever heard. As I was preparing to write this chapter, I thought a lot about what I wanted to say. Talking about sex can be awkward and I didn't want that to be the case with this book. I do, however, want to stress how important sex is in a marriage. I fear there are several married couples today that have the same point of view about sex that our little cousin had. They have no idea the importance of it and because of that, it is not going well. Regardless of what you may have heard, or even what your sex life looks like now, sex is not an awful or awkward or casual thing. It's a beautiful thing created to be shared by two people in the unity of marriage. Most marriages end for one of two reasons- money issues or unfilled sexual issues. This is so very sad because, with the proper attention, both issues can be resolved if the couple chooses to do so. We're going to finish up this chapter talking about how to passionately pursue your spouse in an intimate way. Let's start by seeing what the Bible has to say about the topic.

Sex is a good thing!

Marriage is to be held in honor among all [that is, regarded as something of great value], and the marriage bed undefiled [by immorality or by any sexual sin]; for God will judge the sexually immoral and adulterous.

HEBREWS 13:4 AMPLIFIED VERSION

This is a very interesting time to be married in my opinion. Our society tells us marriage is of no importance. You can marry as often as you want and then just get a divorce if it doesn't work out. Sex is also something of little value in our world right now. Just grab a magazine or watch a tv show, everywhere we look we are shown people sleeping with as many people as possible and basically getting praised for it. In fact, now if you don't sleep around you are looked at as being naive and ridiculed for that. On the flip side, our Christian culture likes to tell us sex is a bad thing. In fact, most churches don't address sex at all, not even in the bonds of marriage. It's something you just don't talk about. But in the above verse, God tells us marriage should be held in a place of honor and sex should only take place between a husband and a wife. It's only when sex happens outside of that relationship that it's a bad thing. Sex is not meant to be casual. It's meant to be a special bond you only share with your spouse.

It's unfortunate most churches don't want to talk about sex because that's all the world wants to talk about. That's why so many people have a warped view of sex and marriage. The church tells them sex is bad by either saying that or not talking about it at all and the world tells us it's amazing and that it's bad to only be with one person. The consequences of that are so very evident in our world today. People are sleeping with everyone like it's no big deal. Sex is not viewed as a gift to be shared in marriage, but as something that can be used when the opportunity arises with whoever happens to be available. Sex has many purposes, but one of those purposes is for the unity, commitment, and enjoyment between two people that are married. Sex is a good gift we are to share in marriage alone.

How's Your Sex Life?

So, let's get really personal for a moment. How is your sex life? Are both you and your spouse happy with what is happening in your bedroom right now? Are things awesome or is there room for improvement? Is it exciting or mundane? Does it happen often or hardly ever? Do both people initiate it or is it the same person all the time? Are you trying new things or just doing the same things over and over? I know these questions can cause people to turn red, but these are the questions that need to be addressed between a married couple. Like I said earlier, some marriages end because one or both people in the relationship have unmet sexual needs. They don't find fulfillment at home, so they go somewhere else to find it. Sex in a marriage should be fun and fulfilling for both people. In fact, the Bible tells us that it should be enjoyable.

> *Now, about sex and marriage: Drink only the water that comes from your own well, and don't let your water flow out into the streets. Keep it for yourself, and don't share it with strangers. Be happy with your own wife. Enjoy the woman you married while you were young. She is like a beautiful deer, a lovely fawn. Let her love satisfy you completely. Stay drunk on her love, and don't go stumbling into the arms of another woman.*
> PROVERBS 5:15-20 EASY READ VERSION

This is Tara Payne's translation of those verses. "When it comes to sex with your spouse- don't stop- get it, get it!" Seriously, read the verses again, is that not what it's saying? It tells us to "stay drunk on the love of our spouse". Alex and I had a person in our lives tells us this one time. "If you're married, it's legal and moral, go for it." In other words, all bets are off. In the unity of marriage, you and your spouse can be as spontaneous and creative as you want to be. So, if that is the case, why are so many couples having issues in this area?

I know some couples have physical problems that may be negatively affecting their sex life. Then, there are some people that have been led to believe that sex only has one purpose and enjoyment is not that purpose. I personally think most of the problems in this area come from one or both people in the relationship not being intentional. They are being passive instead of active in this area and because of that their sex life is suffering. It's time to enjoy the gift you have been given in marriage. It's time to bring some life back to this area. Let's talk about some ways to be intentional about shifting into high gear and passionately pursuing our spouses intimately.

- Start Outside of the Bedroom

One problem I have seen in some couples is they think intimacy only takes place in the bedroom when sex begins. They don't make it a point to show any kind of affection either verbally or physically unless sex is their goal. I know, especially for women, this is not a good thing. Women tend to see sex as more of an emotional experience than just a physical one. There is a lot more that goes into getting us in the mood than just going at it. If we have had a hard day and our spouses haven't shown us any kind of attention, sex probably isn't the first thing on our minds. It's easy to get in the mindset that your spouse just wants to use you for sex, if that's the only time, they show you that kind of attention. That may not be the truth, but it's easier to believe a lie if we aren't careful about it. We need to decide every day to show our spouse some type of intimacy other than only when sex is desired. We need to kiss, hug, and say sweet things just because we care about them and want them to realize that. If we take the time to show affection daily it will help with our sex lives as well. Again, this is especially true with women. If you show us you can be affectionate on a daily basis, when it comes time to have sex, we will be way more willing than if no affection has been shown at all. Another way you can improve your love life before you get into the bedroom is by lightening the other person's load. I am speaking mainly to men with this section and I realize that (don't worry, men, I will talk to the ladies also) but women are interesting creatures. We can't just turn our brains off when there are a lot of things to be done. This may sound silly, but helping your wife wash the dishes could pay off for you later. It really is the small things that add up with us. If you help us with things that are on our mind, it frees us up to focus more on being present and fully participating during sex. So, start in the morning if you want to have sex at night. Show affection daily and do things that will help her out throughout the day. If you are intentional about this, I promise things will shift in your favor.

- Make it Fun

If you are married all bets are off. If both people are comfortable, there are no limits to what you can do with your spouse. So why not try all the things in all the places. I'm talking to you, ladies! Typically, we're the ones that want to hold back in this area. Men are usually down for anything, at any time. Be spontaneous and creative! Put on the tiny lacy outfit. Take it outside of the bedroom. Do something that will totally knock him off his feet. Ladies let's not get passive when it comes to this. It's so easy to let life happen and by the time you are with your spouse you are exhausted, so you just go through the motions or worse, you don't have sex at all. I get it and I have been there. So, let's get better at this together, be intentional, plan it out ahead of time. Go pull the cute outfit out of the back of your closet or go buy something new. Anything that will bring some fun and excitement back to that part of your marriage. Men are very visual, so by making a few little deliberate choices we can totally turn our men on. Not only will your spouse be so excited, but you might find it makes things more enjoyable for you as well. It will be a win-win for everyone.

- Talk about It

The main way you can pursue your spouse passionately is by knowing what they like and then doing that. It doesn't have to be a guessing game, if we want to know what our spouse's favorite color or favorite sports team is, we ask them. The only reason Alex drove me all over the country looking for a bear was I communicated with him that I wanted to see a bear. So why not ask them what they like in other areas. It might be an awkward conversation, but it could completely change your sex life! Some of the things I know about Alex, I only know because either he flat out told me, or I asked. It's ok for you and your spouse to have these conversations, but after you talk, act! If they have mentioned something, try it. I'll say it again, if you are married all bets are off. As long as it won't get you arrested, I say go for it! Sex doesn't have to be a guessing game or a "do the same thing over and over again" game. Talk to each other and learn everything you can about each other. Then go have a great time with each other.

Talking about sex to each other can also help in making it more fun. Alex and I did a 31-day marriage devotion a while back. It gave you an action to do every day to draw you closer to your spouse. On one of the days, the action was to have sex. We knew what was going to happen that night, so all day, we talked about it and texted each other about it. Because we keep bringing it up, it stayed on our minds all day. You would think knowing something was going to happen would make it less exciting, but because we knew, talked about it, and anticipated it, we were both on the same page when the time came. There is nothing wrong with talking about sex with your spouse. It might spice things up if you start talking about it more.

Grinding Gears

Never Use Sex as a Form of Punishment

The husband must fulfill his [marital] duty to his wife [with goodwill and kindness], and likewise the wife to her husband. The wife does not have [exclusive] authority over her own body, but the husband shares with her, and likewise, the husband does not have [exclusive] authority over his body, but the wife shares with him. Do not deprive each other [of marital rights], except perhaps by mutual consent for a time, so that you may devote yourselves [unhindered] to prayer but come together again so that Satan will not tempt you [to sin] because of your lack of self-control.

1 Corinthians 7:3-5 Amplified Version

Have you ever ridden with someone who doesn't know how to drive a manual car? The sound that happens when they put the car in the wrong gear is awful, isn't it? Not only is it awful, but if you continue driving with it in the wrong gear it can totally mess up the car's transmission. Repairing a transmission is a long and expensive process. The same thing happens in a marriage when we make the choice to use sex as leverage. Sex is a gift, not a prize, and only harm will come to your relationship if it's used incorrectly, very expensive harm that will take time to fix. Not only is it unhealthy to withhold sex from your spouse, but the Bible flat out tells us not to do this. The verses in 1 Corinthians tells us to not deprive each other unless it's for a purpose that is mutually agreed upon. Sex is a gift that comes with being married. It is not something that has to be earned. It's not fair to your spouse to hold this as some kind of prize you get only when you have good days. We're not in elementary school on some kind of point system. I know there will be times one of you will not want to be intimate and that's fine. There may be times you don't have sex because of a mutual agreement, like fasting or a health issue, but never say no as a way of hurting your spouse. I'm not going to go on and on about this one. The long and short of this one is, don't do it. This is very harmful to a marriage, and the few times I've seen this done in marriage, the result has never been good. If you are having problems, do everything in your power to work them out, but do not use sex as leverage. What is true about the gears in a car is true with marriage. If you grind your gears long enough damage will happen and the repairs will be long and expensive. Save yourself a lot of trouble and use your gears correctly.

Never Stop Finding Ways to Pursue Your Spouse

Through this chapter, I hope you have learned there are multiple ways to pursue your spouse every day both inside and outside of the bedroom by just making a few shifts in your choices and your actions. Passionate pursue is not limited to just one area of your life but can be a part of every moment. I encourage you to make the daily the deliberate. Find ways every day to passionately pursue your spouse. Don't fall into the trap of being passive about them and passionate about something or someone else. It's time to stop being idle and to shift whatever gear we need to shift in order to actively pursue our spouse and love them in a passionate way. We all have a passion within us. Let's turn that passion upward to the Lord and outward to our spouses. Let's pursue them like I pursed that bear- loud, wild, and without restraint! Let the gear shifting begin!

CHAPTER 6

THE ENGINE
(FAITHFULNESS AND LOYALTY)

Life is a journey only the faithful and loyal last the distance
~ author unknown

I absolutely love the above quote. It's so simple yet so profound and encouraging. I personally want to go the distance on this adventure of marriage. I want to be the couple that grows ridiculously old together. I want Alex and I to be the couple that is more in love in our 90's than we are now in our 30's. I want to be the old couple still holding hands in public. I want to look back on my marriage, years down the road and know I gave it my all and, because of that, I have no regrets. I want a beautiful adventure. And I can have all that and so can you! At this point, you are roughly halfway through the book and I pray I have conveyed that marriage takes work, but it's so worth it. I hope you are encouraged and spurred on to put in the work necessary to make your marriage a beautiful adventure. I hope you see a good marriage is possible. You may not be where you want to be now but stay the course friends. If you give your marriage your all God will honor that.

Forsaking all Others and Keeping Myself Only to You

Then I will take you for My people, and I will be your God; and you shall know that I am the Lord your God, who redeemed you and brought you out from under the burdens of the Egyptians.

EXODUS 6:7 AMPLIFIED VERSION

In this chapter, we are going to dive into what it means to be faithful and loyal to your spouse. Faithfulness and loyalty are fleeting character traits these days. People say their vows, and, in some cases, they never intend on keeping them. They are just words to be repeated but hold no promise or commitment. How sad is it that some people go into a marriage with the mindset they can still do anything or have anyone they want? I believe our vows should be taken seriously. We have talked earlier about how marriage is a model of Christ and His church. Our marriages are meant to show the love Christ has for His bride. The husband leading the wife and loving her unconditionally and the wife submitting to her husband by respecting and honoring him. The Lord can use our marriages to model many of His attributes if we will just honor our vows.

One thing we can model in our marriage is the faithfulness of God. If you go back to the Old Testament you will see where God chose the Children of Israel to be His people. He made a covenant with them. He promised them He would be their God and they would be His people. God chose them just like we choose the person we marry and then He spoke a vow over them that He would never leave them or forsake them. Basically, it was a marriage ceremony. Not many people talk about the story of the Children of Israel as showing a marriage model, but it really is a beautiful story between God and His bride. He made a vow then put it into practice. Ever since He made that covenant with her, He has been doing everything with the intention of drawing His bride to Himself by showing His faithfulness to her. Even when she was acting a fool. He never left her. He never picked another bride. He remained and still remains faithful to her. That's some amazing love. That is also some great news for us. When we get saved, we become a part of this beautiful love story. We become the bride of Christ which means His faithfulness is now extended to us. He has never walked away from His bride, which means He will never walk away from us!

So, what should we do with this great love and faithfulness we have been given? We should show great love and faithfulness to our spouse. We have been given a great opportunity to help further God's kingdom and His love in a dying world by portraying marriage in a Biblical light. We get to show God's faithfulness and love in our marriages. We get to show this world vows are important. That faithfulness to one person is possible and beautiful. When I started viewing my marriage as a platform in which I could further God's Kingdom, it shifted my perspective in some areas. Marriage is a ministry. We "get to" be a part of His master plan to save the world. What a privilege we have been given. And we get to do all these things with our best friend, that's even better!

Gentlemen, Start Your Engines

So, if we're going to walk out this calling let's start with the basics, what does it mean to be faithful and loyal? According to Wikipedia~ *Faithfulness is the concept of unfailingly remaining loyal to someone or something and putting that loyalty into consistent practice regardless of extenuating circumstances. It may be exhibited by a husband or wife who, in a sexually exclusive marriage, do not engage in sexual relationships outside of the marriage. Loyal is a strong feeling of support or allegiance.* Faithfulness and loyalty mean to choose your spouse over everyone else. Then you continue to choose them every single day just like the Lord does with us. Faithfulness and loyalty mean you honor your vows and live your life in a way that fulfills them. When I was thinking about what I could compare faithfulness and loyalty to I asked myself what was something physical that would be highly important for an adventure. Something you would have to choose to take good care of and maintain if it was going to go the distance. We have talked about the driver, the navigator, the tires, and the gears so far. Faithfulness and loyalty are so important for a marriage to be successful. It had to be something crucial for an adventure. Then it hit me! The engine! If you don't take good care of the engine of whatever form of transportation you choose, you aren't going anywhere. Not only must you take care of your engine, but you also can't allow the wrong things to get inside of your engine. You can't fill it with junk. It must stay pure and clean if it's going to power the rest of the vehicle. So let's spend some time talking about ways we can take care of the engine of our marriage by being faithful and loyal to our spouse and let's also talk about some things we may be putting in our engines that may seem innocent, but can hinder that faithfulness and loyalty.

To Have and To Hold

So, run away from sexual sin. It involves the body in a way that no other sin does. So, if you commit sexual sin, you are sinning against your own body

1 CORINTHIANS 6:18 EASY READ VERSION

Let's start with the most obvious way to stay faithful to your spouse. When we stand before God, and the people we have invited to our wedding, we make the promise "to have and to hold" our spouse from this time forward. That means we promise we will only be in a sexual relationship with them. They should be the only person that gets our engines revving! They are going to be the only oil we choose for our engines for the rest of our lives! To me, this is a beautiful thing. I personally love the fact that I will only be with Alex for the rest of my life and he will only be with me. By honoring this vow, it deepens our relationship and adds a layer of trust and commitment that would not be there if we shared these same intimate moments with other people. It creates a soul tie between us that is exclusive to us. By honoring this vow, it's a physical promise that says, "I choose you and only you forever". When we make this decision, and then continue to do so, it's great for our engines. When we make this choice, it helps our engine to stay clean, healthy and to run smoothly because it's being taken care of.

However, a lot of people have mixed points of view about this one. In fact, some people don't even want to be married because they think being with only one person would be very boring. They want to try out all the oils. I know of married couples that say they have "open" relationships. They are together, but also sleep with other people. I honestly can't even wrap my brain around what these couples are thinking. Mixing oils is not good for a literal engine and it's especially not good for our relational engines! In 1 Corinthians it tells us to run away from sexual immorality. It doesn't say to be careful with it. It doesn't say it's ok every now and then. It says to run away from it. When I think about running away from something, I think about putting as much distance as possible between me, and whatever it is, I'm running away from. I think about it being very dangerous and, because of that, I should not be even remotely close to it. So, when I read that verse, I see the Lord speaking through Paul warning us very urgently to stay away from a situation that can cause us great harm.

This is not the only time God talks about the dangers of sexual immorality. It's mentioned several times throughout the Bible and in every context, we are warned to stay away from it because of the danger it will bring. Anytime something is mentioned more than once in the Bible we really need to sit up and take notice. If He is being super verbal about something it means He really wants us to get it! It's not the Lord being repetitive for no purpose. It's the Lord trying to seriously convey to us the importance of a topic. Having sex with multiple people is dangerous not only to us but everyone involved. If you put the wrong oil into your engine it will cause problems and if those problems aren't dealt with it can damage the engine. If we're not faithful and loyal to our spouses, it will cause problems and damage to our marriages.

Soul Ties

Do you not know that the one who joins himself to a prostitute is one body with her? For He says, "The two shall be one flesh."
1 Corinthians 6:16 Amplified Version

So, what makes having sex with multiple people so dangerous? Obviously, there is the danger of getting a sexually transmitted disease and, in turn, giving it to your spouse, but that's not the danger the Bible is talking about when it says to stay away from sexual immorality. The danger of sex with multiple people goes way deeper than any physical disease we could contract. In the above verse, it tells us what the real danger is. When we have sex with other people, we become one with them. There is a union that happens physically but there is also a union that happens spiritually whether we intend for it to or not. That union is called a soul tie. According to google a soul tie is," A *spiritual connection between two people who have been physically intimate with each other or who have had an intensely emotional or spiritual association or relationship.*" God designed sex to create a soul tie because it was only supposed to happen between a husband and wife. When it comes to our spouses this is a great thing. When we commit to only being intimate with our spouse, the soul tie created serves to strengthen us because it bonds us together on a deeper spiritual level. In layman's terms, it's like a layer of reinforced glue that helps to hold us tightly together. When we only have sex with our spouses and that soul tie stays intact it's an amazing and God-glorifying thing.

The problem with these soul ties outside of marriage is the people having sex are creating these bonds but aren't staying together. I have heard it described like this. When we glue two objects together, they become one. As long as they stay glued together, they are both wholes. But what happens when we tear those two things apart? It damages both pieces, right? When the glue is applied, then ripped off, both sides are altered in some way. It's never a clean break. There are always pieces missing and pieces left behind. The same thing happens with us when we sleep around. There is no such thing as casual sex. A soul tie is created with every sexual encounter we have. When those two people go their separate ways, pieces are left behind, and the damage is done. Soul ties bind us to the people we have been with and potentially any junk they may be dealing with as well. It is like an all-access pass for both parties. Because we are bound to these people it may cause us to continue to have feelings for them that open the door for unfaithfulness on multiple levels. These ties need to be broken so we can be free to experience a strong bond with only our spouses.

God designed sex so a husband and wife could come together in the bonds of marriage and become one both physically and spiritually. A soul tie with your spouse will be the glue that keeps you closely connected. Do not fall into the dangers of having sex outside of your marriage. It won't only destroy your marriage, but it will destroy you as well.

All Things New

Therefore if anyone is in Christ [that is, grafted in, joined to Him by faith in Him as Savior], he is a new creature [reborn and renewed by the Holy Spirit]; the old things [the previous moral

and spiritual condition] have passed away. Behold, new things
have come [because spiritual awakening brings a new life].

2 CORINTHIANS 5:17 AMPLIFIED VERSION

Before we leave the topic of soul ties, I want to leave you with some encouragement. If you have had sex with other people besides your spouse, whether it was before you were married or after, and those other soul ties exist, they can be broken off you by repenting, renouncing, and refilling. These three steps will help you to clean out your engines spiritually. Bring them before the Lord and repent of them first. Ask Him to forgive you of your past unfaithfulness and sexual immorality. Renounce your past by speaking it out loud to the Lord. In Jesus' name ask Him to break any soul tie that exists off you. Tell Him you want to commit to only being with your spouse and you want that soul tie to be the only one left intact. Then ask Him to refill you. Ask Him to fill that space where the soul tie was with His Spirit and to give you a desire for only your spouse. Ask Him to strengthen the bond between you and your spouse in every possible way. Soul ties are powerful, but our God is more powerful. We must use our words and go through all three steps- repeat, renounce, and refill- to have those unholy ties broken off us.

We serve a God that makes all things new. He can break those unholy soul ties and do a spiritual clean up. He can and will give you a fresh new engine. You can have that unity with your spouse and no other regardless of the mistakes you have made in the past. We serve a merciful, forgiving, and restorative God. It's not too late to have that special bond with only your spouse. Our God makes all things new and that includes our engines. Hallelujah!

Be Careful Little Eyes What You See

Watch over your heart with all diligence, for from it flow the springs of life.

PROVERBS 4:23 AMPLIFIED VERSION

Being faithful to your spouse has many facets. We have talked about the most obvious one which is to not have literal sex with other people but let's dive a little deeper into other ways we can stay faithful to our spouse. I personally believe when God designed marriage, He designed it to be a relationship where one man and one woman commit to being with each other and only each other in every way. We are to find sexual fulfillment with one person and one person only and, contrary to what our society tells us, that is totally possible. So, with that in mind, one way we can remain faithful to our spouse and keep our engines clean is by staying away from all forms of pornographic material. Now you may have read that sentence and thought, "Viewing porn is not cheating on my spouse! It's a magazine or a video. It's not an actual person I'm having an actual relationship with, so how is that being unfaithful to my spouse? How is that dangerous to me and my marriage?" Well, I'm very glad that you asked those questions.

Mark Gungor is a pastor that focuses on marriage and relationships. He does teachings on the dangers of porn that are very fascinating. I highly encourage you to look him up because he goes in depth on the subject. I want to take a little time and touch on a little bit of what he teaches here about how porn can affect us and our relationship negatively.

I am my beloved's, and his desire is for me.

SONG OF SOLOMON 7:10 AMPLIFIED VERSION

In Song of Solomon, we find this exchange between two people who are in love. If you think the Bible is boring clearly you haven't read Song of Solomon. In this passage, the couple is proclaiming all the things they love about each other and they talk about how they find enjoyment and pleasure in each other's bodies. In the above verse, the lady is speaking and telling us her beloved's desires are toward her. Let's really think about what she is saying with this short verse. She knows he's attracted to her and pursues her. She knows she gets his engine revving! She is confident in the fact that he thinks she is the hottest thing ever and he wants to be with only her. She is confident about all these things. Why? Because that is the message that he is constantly conveying to her by his words and actions. He is saying the right things and then validating his words with his actions.

Honestly, isn't that what we all want? We all want to be desired by our spouses. We want them to think we are the hottest thing ever. We want to be pursued by them. We want them to be turned on by us. We want to be the only object of their affection. We want to be the only person that gets their engine revving! And there is absolutely nothing wrong with wanting this! Being pursued by Alex, and knowing he wants to be with me exclusively is such a wonderful feeling. We often tell each other, "I choose you." Much like the verse above, it is a seemingly simple little declaration, but it holds so much power in our relationship. Because Alex's words and actions convey the same message, it gives me so much confidence. However, regardless of the words you use, you can't give your spouse this kind of confidence if you are choosing to look at porn.

When you choose to look at porn it shifts your desires to someone or something else. When you start looking at porn you are choosing that over your spouse. You are non-verbally saying your spouse is not good enough. You are non-verbally saying your spouse is not sexy enough. You are non-verbally saying you would rather be with a piece of paper or a video than be with your spouse. Now would you literally come out and say those things to the person you married? I would surely hope not, however, when you choose to view porn that is the declaration you are making, and if your spouse is aware of this, that is the message they are hearing loud and clear. That may seem like a harsh statement, but it's the truth. In most cases, actions speak louder than words, so when we decide to view porn we're choosing and desiring someone or something over the one we married and that is what we are communicating to them.

There are so many ways this can hurt our marriages. If your spouse is not aware of the situation then deception enters the equation. We aren't being faithful to our spouses because we're turning our desires to something else and then lying to them about that part of our lives. The enemy can do so much with a lie. He tells us it's ok to lie, but then, as soon as we do, he brings in guilt and shame. He tells us we can't stop, but then condemns us when we continue to do the exact things he encouraged. Once lies enter a relationship they tend to just grow and grow. One lie leads to another lie which leads to another lie. With lying comes a lack of trust and trust is so important in a good marriage.

Now if your spouse does know about the situation, that doesn't make it any better. Then the spirit of resentment and comparison comes into the equation. Women struggle so much with comparison anyway, but the enemy can really mess with them if their husbands are viewing porn. Everywhere a woman looks there are magazines, ads, and tv shows telling them all the things they need to do to have the perfect body and life. Everywhere we turn we see images of the perfect woman. So just on a normal day, it's easy to fall into the trap of comparison and inadequacy, but when you go home to the person that is supposed to love you unconditionally, the person that says they chose you, and find they are choosing to look at other women, it's heartbreaking. The declaration of, "you are not enough," will ring loud and clear in a woman's ear when her husband chooses porn over her. This spirit of comparison then, in turn, can bring up other nasty emotions that can wreak havoc on a relationship.

The same is true for men. Men struggle with comparison as much as women do. It's just not talked about as much. So, wives, if you're the one looking at porn the same rules apply, you are communicating to your man that he is not enough. The message of, "you are not enough," is never the message that we should be communicating to our spouses. That message will never bring life to a relationship-only death. It doesn't matter who's communicating it or receiving it, the result will be the same.

Imitation Stimulation

Porn is not only dangerous to your relationship; it's also dangerous to the person that is viewing it. Porn is just like a drug, it's addictive. The more you watch, the more you want to watch. The more you watch, the more time you spend away from actual people and normal relationships. I have read several blogs on the topic and the findings are fascinating. Watching porn can alter your brain. It can alter the way your body responds to stimuli and the chemicals your body produces. Because of these alterations, people who view porn get desensitized to actual sexual experiences. Their bodies get regimented to a certain stimulus so that is the only one it wants to respond too. Really stop and think about that for a moment. Porn can literally change the way our bodies respond sexually. As I read the blogs about it, I couldn't help but feel sympathy for the people that have fallen victim to this. They have become slaves to this, to the detriment of themselves, and don't even realize it.

> Now the Lord God said, "It is not good (beneficial) for the man to be alone; I will make him a helper [one who balances him—a counterpart who is suitable and complimentary for him.]
> GENESIS 2:18 AMPLIFIED VERSION

God created us to be community driven. When God created Adam, He said it wasn't good for Adam to be alone, so He created Eve. We need to be with other people. We need a smile or a loving touch from someone. We need those intimate moments with other people whether that be sex or just a conversation. Even people who are more introverted need some kind of social interaction from time to time. It's just the way God wired us to be. So, when someone chooses porn, they are choosing something other than actual human contact. They are choosing an imitation over the real thing and the imitation is never as good. Like I said earlier, porn changes the way the human body responds to other stimuli, so when all we give it is an imitation, that's all it will want. When an encounter with a real person happens, our body doesn't respond the way it was designed to because it has been programed to accept the imitation.

Mark Gungor calls it artificial stimulation. When we view porn, we actually train our brains to only respond to a magazine or a computer screen instead of with our spouses. It breaks the connection with our spouse because we no longer get fulfillment with them. When fulfillment doesn't happen with our spouses, we may stop trying to find it with them all together and we go to the place where we think we are getting fulfilled, but again, it's not true fulfillment, it's artificial. Because it's artificial, we must continually come back to it for that feeling we long for, but here lies the problem. The same porn that once worked for us doesn't work after a while, so we must go deeper and darker into it to find that feeling we are craving. We must view it more and more often to get that feeling. This causes the person to isolate themselves more and more. This causes the person to spend more time in front of their computer screen than with their spouse. This causes the person to dive into things they would never consider watching or doing before just because they are looking for a feeling of fulfillment. It's here in those times of isolation the enemy can do his best work. Isolation breeds guilt and shame for the person viewing the porn. The isolation the spouse experiences breeds comparison, inadequacy, and resentment. With those feelings comes division in marriage.

If someone tried to sell you imitation oil for your car, I'm sure you would turn them down. We would never put subpar oil into our actual engines because we know it wouldn't work as well as the real oil or be good for the health of our engines. Yet so many people do this with their marriages when they choose porn over their spouse. Porn is a form of unfaithfulness and it's so very dangerous to the person viewing it, the spouse, and the marriage. The good news is, there is hope for the person who has chosen the imitation over the real thing. I encourage you to look up Mark Gungor and all his sermons and studies on this topic. He goes more in-depth, and he also goes into how to retrain your brain and ways to get away from the artificial stimulation and find true fulfillment with your spouse. If you have fallen into this trap be encouraged there is a way out. You can find fulfillment with your spouse again.

Be Careful Little Mouth What You Say

Do not let unwholesome [foul, profane, worthless, vulgar] words ever come out of your mouth, but only such speech as is good for building up others, according to the need and the occasion, so that it will be a blessing to those who hear [you speak].

EPHESIANS 4:49 AMPLIFIED VERSION

I want to finish up this chapter on faithfulness and loyalty by talking about two ways we can be faithful and loyal to our spouses with our words. Our words are very powerful. I believe all of us take for granted just how truly powerful words can be and that's why I have spent so much time in this book talking about our words. Ask anyone if they can recall words that have been spoken over them or to them that have impacted them either positive or negative and they can give you an example almost instantly. People's lives have been altered entirely by words spoken to them. There are people who have accomplished great things because someone spoke life to them and there are others who have done nothing because someone spoke death over them. We hold the same power with the words we speak over our marriages and our spouses. We can change the trajectory of our marriage by changing our words.

Several years ago, I went to the wedding of two amazing people the Lord has put in my life, Ronnie and Michelle Harman. The vows Michelle spoke to Ronnie have never left me because they were so unique. They didn't do the traditional vows. They wrote their own. One of the things she said to him that day was, "Your name is safe in my mouth." When I first heard it, I was a little confused. I really didn't know what that meant. Later she explained to me that it was a promise to never bad mouth him to anyone, in any way. She went on to explain how easy it is to fall into the habit of speaking negatively about your spouse especially if others are doing it and how they had both made a promise to never do that. She took the promise so seriously she made it a part of her vows. I have known this couple for years and I send a lot of time with them and I have never heard them speak negatively about each other in all that time. "Your name is safe in my mouth." Such a small sentence but when applied in our marriage it holds such power for us.

In marriage we get to see the good, the bad, and the ugly but this doesn't give us permission to use our words as a weapon against our spouses. We need to remain faithful to our spouses by making sure that their name is safe with us. There is so much negativity in this world, we need to be their safe place. A place they can be themselves without fear of being exposed. Being faithful in this area is two-fold, we will have to watch our words, but we may also have to distance ourselves from others who speak negatively about their spouses. Negative begets negative. If you stay around for those negative conversations, you are more susceptible to engage in it. In those situations, try to change where the conversation is going but if you can't change it, leave it. Better to walk away than to break a promise and be unfaithful with your words.

Let's Take it Further

Let's take it a step further shall we? Not only should we not speak negatively about our spouses, we shouldn't speak more highly of someone else to others either. We don't need to talk about how hot another man or woman is to our friends all the time. I know married people who speak more highly and often of a movie star than they do their own spouses. I know people who spend more time flirting with the people that come into their jobs and then talking to their co-workers about how cute they are than they do their own spouses. I'm sure I am stepping on some toes now and you may think I'm taking it way too far. Am I? Have you really stopped to think this through? Is this really harmless? I feel very strongly this kind of talk is unhealthy for a marriage. What are we really saying when we make those comments? We are saying someone is better in some way than our spouses. That is the underlying message we are conveying. Someone is hotter, someone is smarter, someone is just better!

Two things happen when we engage in these conversations. One, it leaves the one speaking it with discontentment. We start to think about all the ways this other person is better and how our spouses fall short. This opens the door for the enemy to come in and confirm all these thoughts. Our thoughts turn into words and our words turn into actions. If we aren't careful, we start treating our spouses poorly because we feel like they aren't good enough. Think about that. If you spend all your time talking about how good someone else is, when you get home to your spouse, you aren't going to treat them kindly because you have spent your day focused on their shortcomings. You have put a magnifying glass on the wrong things, so your focus is off. The second danger is this kind of talk brings with it the spirit of comparison for your spouse. If they know you make these comments, and most of the time they do to some extent, they could start comparing themselves to that other person which could make them feel inadequate. So now not only are you seeing all these "supposed" flaws, but they start seeing them also. When comparison and discontentment come into marriage, problems are sure to follow. These problems can be avoided in marriage altogether by just making the decision to remain faithful to your spouse with your words.

> *Death and life are in the power of the tongue, and those who love it and indulge it will eat its fruit and bear the consequences of their words.*
> PROVERBS 18:21 AMPLIFIED VERSION

Alex and I have had several conversations on this topic. Now, do we believe there is anything wrong with acknowledging someone looks nice or has done something noteworthy? No, there is nothing wrong with that at all. Those aren't the comments I'm talking about. There is a difference in saying someone looked very nice today, and moving on, versus talking endlessly about how hot someone is all the time. I get that this seems harmless because everyone seems to do this, but I assure you it's not harmless, and it will only bring unnecessary problems to your relationship. Proverbs tells us life and death are in our words. We can bring life or death to our marriages with our words. We can build up or we can tear down. The choice is ours to make!

This topic has been in the front of my mind for about a year now. I see other couples making remarks about other people in front of their spouses and honestly it breaks my heart. I feel sorry for the other person because I know how it would make me feel if Alex went around talking about how hot other women were. Most of the time it's about some movie star and I understand they are never going to run off with them but still. Whether or not the other person is obtainable is irrelevant. It's the way you are making your spouse feel and what you're choosing to focus on that's the true issue here. I choose my words carefully when it comes to Alex because he deserves that. I want him to have the same confidence he has given me. We take this very seriously, some would say to seriously, but because we have taken it so seriously there is not discontentment or comparison in our marriage. I know Alex is faithful to me in his words and his actions so that is one area the enemy has no power. Don't give the enemy a foothold to cause division and the opportunity for unfaithfulness in your marriage. It's simply not worth it. Your spouse deserves kind words spoken to them and about them!

Be the Change

Do you know how affairs usually happen? Typically, it's a process and it starts by having a conversation with a person. It starts out innocently enough, but the more you talk, the more information you share. As you share information, a deeper relationship forms, then you start talking about things you should only talk about with your spouse. Then you start talking about all the issues you have with your spouse. You start seeing this other person as perfect, with no shortcomings, and all you see is the shortcomings of the one you married. Before you know it, you want to be with this other person more and more until an affair happens. That is the usual progression, no one just wakes up one day and thinks it's a good day to be unfaithful. It starts with a, "Hey, how are you?", and goes from there. By having these conversations with other people, the ones we should only have with our spouses, we are opening the door for so many problems, major problems that have caused many marriages to crumble.

We can avoid this altogether by always choosing our spouses. Go to them first. Only share certain conversations with them. The conversations about your marriage, your family, your finances, and your future should only be shared in the intimacy of a married relationship. Your spouse is the person you're on this adventure with and they are the only one that should get all the details. They should be the only ones that make the decisions on how the adventure should look. They should know if you are happy, sad, or upset before anyone else. They should be the one to help you make the hard decisions. Friends are awesome and so important. We need outside opinions sometimes, but not on everything. Keep your friends wide but only go deep when it comes to your spouse.

Therefore, since we are surrounded by so great a cloud of witnesses [who by faith have testified to the truth of God's absolute faithfulness], stripping off every unnecessary weight and the sin which so easily and cleverly entangles us, let us run with endurance and active persistence the race that is set before us,
HEBREWS 12:1 AMPLIFIED VERSION

There are so many things the world tells us are ok that will stall our engines or completely destroy them if we allow them into our marriages. Adultery, porn, and careless words are just the three we talked about in this chapter. The good news is we can make a choice not to let these things affect our engines, and if we already have, we can get a tune-up and our engines can run smoothly again. Remember what I said in chapter four, God is the master mechanic. We can overcome anything the enemy throws at us because of the power of Jesus that is inside of us. We can be faithful and loyal to our spouses if we make the choice and become very intentional about it. With God's help, our marriage adventure can run smoothly, and our lives can be restored.

On this adventure, let's make a choice to remain faithful and loyal to our spouses in every possible way. Let's make a choice to be a model of God's faithfulness to a world that is falling apart at the seams. Let's make small decisions every day that will have a big impact on our lives, our marriages, and this world. The world needs to see that marriage is a good thing. The world needs to see you can be happily married to one person and be faithful to them. The world needs to see that porn is not helpful or necessary but dangerous and isolating. The world needs to see the beauty of one man and one woman committing to have and to hold only each other and no one or nothing else. The world needs to see a man and a woman bragging about their spouse instead of ripping them apart. Everything you do and say should convey the same message to your spouse. "You are the only person that gets my engine revving!" Ask yourself if that is the message you are conveying with your words and your actions. If it isn't, change it! Today is the day! We can be that model. We can be the catalyst for change in this world by using our actions and our words for God's glory to shine in our marriage. Don't follow the crowd, be the shift, be the change, be faithful and loyal. Let's take it too far and change the world.

CHAPTER 7

THE KEYS (CONSISTENCY)

Once you have tasted flight, you will forever walk the earth with
your eyes turned skyward, for there you have been,
and there you will always long to return.
~ Leonardo da Vinci

There we were on a hot June morning; Alex and I were standing in front of the tiniest plane I think I have ever seen. We had gone through about 5 minutes of training, gotten harnessed up, and now we were waiting to board this plane so it could take us up 15,000 feet, fly us around the Grand Canyon, and then we would skydive. But I'm getting ahead of myself. Let's talk about how we got to this particular adventure before I share with you what the Lord taught me that day.

Alex was approaching his 30th birthday and we were trying to decide what he wanted to do to celebrate it. 30 is one of those milestones everyone looks at with negativity. Apparently, you're officially old when you hit 30 and your life starts going downhill, or at least that's what people have told me. Because of all the negativity around that age, we decided to make our 30th birthdays fun. When I turned 30, we threw a masquerade murder mystery dinner where the guest had to solve a murder. It was so great. When Alex's turn came around, I wanted it to be a big deal also. He told me he wanted to go skydiving on his 30th birthday. So, I started looking into some local places. During this time Alex and Andy started talking about it and Andy suggested if we were going to skydive, we should do it at the Grand Canyon. This totally peaked Alex's interest, he started googling, and found out you could indeed skydive at the Grand Canyon. At that point, I went into plan mode. Alex wanted Penny and Andy to go with us since this had been Andy's idea and they agreed so I called Paragon Skydiving and set up the appointment.

From the moment our reservation was in place this feeling of fear fell over me. What had I done? How did I let this happen? Yes, I "wanted" to skydive because I thought it would be cool, but here I am with reservations to actually do it and now I'm tripping. We had made the plans several months in advance so that meant I had several months of feeling this way. It was as if all my peace had left me. Every time I thought about our upcoming vacation, I would get sick to my stomach. Alex, on the other hand, never had those feelings at all. He's the fearless one in our relationship. He's always down to jump out of something or be shot out of something. The boy is so adventurous, and he was so excited about this trip. Any time I would voice my concerns he would just smile and tell me it was going to be fine. So, let's fast forward to the day before we jumped. We are on our way to the Grand Canyon when I get a call saying that they wanted to move our reservation up to early the next morning because of weather concerns. Great, now we're jumping sooner, again no peace to be found. But this is where the Lord stepped in and did something very cool.

When I woke up the next morning, all the bad feelings were gone and in their place was the feeling of excitement and peace. It was such a strange feeling to experience especially since the last few months had been filled with the opposite feelings. I just kind of brushed it off thinking the bad feelings would come back at some point, but they never did. We arrived at the airport, no fear just peace. We had our 5-minute training, no fear just peace. They put us into this tiny plane with a plastic roll down door closed with Velcro, no fear just peace. It came time to jump, I'm strapped to a complete stranger I met 30 minutes ago and at this point, I'm hanging out of this plane. Literally, my entire body is hanging out of the plane at 15,000 feet in the air as my new friend is looking to make sure we are in the right spot to jump. I was looking out and down over everything and at this moment I should've been completely out of my mind with fear, but it was nowhere to be found. In fact, at that moment I was having the time of my life. And then he let go of the plane and there we went. There are no words that can possibly describe the feeling of skydiving. It was the most mind-blowing experience ever. From start to finish it was great. For a small moment, I knew what it was like to fly and be completely free and now I'm totally hooked. Afterward, I couldn't believe what had happened. Where had the fear gone? Where did that peace come from? The Lord answered these questions by dropping this verse into my heart.

And the peace of God [that peace which reassures the heart, that peace] which transcends all understanding, [that peace which] stands guard over your hearts and your minds in Christ Jesus [is yours].

PHILIPPIANS 4:7 AMPLIFIED VERSION

I have read that particular verse probably a hundred times, but until that moment it had never held that much meaning to me. I just didn't completely grasp what it was saying. Now I have a greater understanding of what that verse means. This verse tells us this indescribable peace is ours. God has already given it to us if we are His, all we must do is tap into it. I experienced a peace that made no sense whatsoever. I should've been afraid, but I wasn't. God used this moment in my life to show me I had that peace in me the whole time. It was literally at my disposal. God did a work in me that day to teach me what was already

115

mine, His peace. A peace I had never experienced before. He solidified this verse in a way I would never forget it. He taught me that when we walk in peace, His peace, it makes all our adventures so much more enjoyable. I would have gone skydiving either way. The reservation had been made and the bill had been paid, but by doing it in a position of peace, it made it one of the greatest adventures of my life. Without that peace, it would've been a horrible experience because I would've been so afraid. I also learned a valuable lesson on trust that day. Peace and trust work best together. The Lord had given me the peace to have an awesome adventure, but if I had not trusted my instructor it still would've ended badly. We had to work together as a team. I had to follow his instructions and not fight against him for us to have fun and land safely. Without trust, peace is rendered ineffective.

We can apply these two lessons in our marriage as well. We must have peace and trust if we're going to enjoy the journey to our desired destination. We have to work together as a team to gain peace and trust. We can't fight against each other and expect things to be peaceful. We can go on this adventure one of two ways. With fear, doubt, and other nasty feelings or we can have peace in our relationships and trust our spouse. We can fight against each other every chance we get and make things more difficult or we can work together as a team with a shared goal. Our adventure can be filled with problems and bad experiences or it can be the adventure of a lifetime. The choice in which we experience, is ours. In this chapter, we are going to be talking about the importance of peace and trust in our marriages, ways to establish and maintain them, and how to build them back up in the event they have been broken. The peace of God is already ours; we just have to put it into action!

Consistency is the Key

You can't take a road trip if you don't have the keys to your car. You could walk, but you wouldn't get very far, and the journey would be harder than it needed to be because you wouldn't be using the tools available to you. Without the proper tools, you would be working harder, but gaining fewer results. Keys are a necessity if you're going to travel easily and go further. Consistency is the key to having a good marriage. Without consistency, anything we do or say will not have the same effect because it will not be fully received. Without consistency doubt and distrust will be present, and with those present, you can't experience true peace and trust. Just like going on a road trip with no keys, having a marriage without consistency is doing double the work with less result. It just makes things harder for no reason at all. So, let's not tire ourselves out, let's not go on the adventure of marriage without the key of consistency. Let's not go on this adventure without the peace and trust that consistency brings.

Peace and trust really do go hand in hand. I had never given it much thought until I jumped out of a plane with a complete stranger, but had I not experienced the peace from God and trusted my instructor, it would not have been a good experience, in fact, it might have actually been a deadly experience, one that ended catastrophically. As I dove deeper into these two subjects, I have come to realize you can't have one without the other. When you trust someone, with that trust, comes peace about that person's actions and motives. When you don't trust them, you won't be at peace because you will constantly be questioning everything they do or don't do. We have marriages that are ending catastrophically because there is no trust and with that lack of trust peace is nowhere to be found. If you and your spouse are children of God, you both already have this peace, you just have to find a way to tap into it as a couple.

I have mentioned several times Alex and I love to travel, and our relationship was founded on adventure. It's just a part of who we are. We are always down for a good road trip. Alex is great at directions and can typically figure out how to get somewhere with or without GPS. When we go somewhere, he studies different ways to get there and takes the time to know exactly where we are going. Because of this, I have full trust that we will arrive at our destination and most of the time I'm so at peace with his abilities I sleep while he drives. Now it didn't start this way. The trust and peace I have in his ability to get us where we are going had to be built over time. How did that peace and trust get established? He consistently got us to our destination. Every adventure we went on, we arrived safely and happily. I came to realize that was an area he never failed in accomplishing. Because of his consistency, trust was born and from that trust, peace was established. By being consistent, peace and trust have now spilled over into other aspects of our marriage. Our words are consistent. Our actions are consistent. So now peace and trust are consistent in our marriage.

Consistency is our key to a beautiful adventure. Consistency is the place where trust and peace are established and where they will thrive. According to google being consistent means *acting or doing something in the same way over time, unchanging in nature or standard.* Let's focus on the "over time" part of this definition for just a moment. Trust and peace are two things that are established over time. You don't just wake up one day and fully and completely trust someone and that includes your spouse. Trust and peace start to form the moment you meet someone and continue to form over time as actions are done the same way.

When Alex and I first started traveling together, I was very proactive in the directions. I wanted to know where we were going, how we were going to get there, where we were during the trip, and how much longer it would take. I was basically your typical kiddo on a road trip. I had all the questions and I was not afraid to ask them multiple times if I deemed it necessary. I know this had to be frustrating to Alex, and at times, I would see some of that frustration, but he would always just answer my questions and then assure me he knew what he was doing, where we were, and that we would get to our destination. Alex's famous statement, that I still hear a lot, is "Tara, I got this." Over time I've come to see he does "have this" and from those consistent moments, trust and peace have been formed and solidified. He has gotten us where we were going over and over, and because of that now I let him handle the directions completely. I very seldom get involved in them at all because I know he has it under control. He has proven to me that, "He's got this!"

Consistency can build trust and peace in every area of your life if we will implement it. By choosing life-giving words, over time, you can build trust and peace in your marriage. By doing what you say you will do over time trust and peace can be established. By showing up every day and doing your best over time trust and peace can be established. Be encouraged that consistency doesn't mean the absence of mistakes it just means the presence of your best effort. Let me explain. We are all going to make mistakes from time to time. Wrong turns happen that can get us off course in our marriages. That is why we had a whole chapter on forgiveness and extending grace. We will be talking about how to rebuild trust and peace after it has been broken shortly. I'm not talking about those big wrong turns right now; I'm just talking about the little mistakes we make from time to time. The main thing here is to always be consistent at doing your best. Has Alex ever made a few wrong turns on our road trips? Yes. But these wrong turns haven't bothered me because I knew he had our destination in mind, and he would get us back on course. The same principle applies in marriage. Detours happen, wrong turns happen, but by consistently doing our best and keeping the final destination in mind, we can enjoy our adventure with peace and trust in one another. Wrong turns and detours will not completely ruin a marriage if a foundation of trust and peace are in place.

Small Steps Over Time Create Big Results

Alex and I have a friend that accomplished a huge goal. He walked the entire Appalachian Trail from start to finish. For those you who are unfamiliar with the Appalachian Trail, it's a 2,190-mile hiking trail that starts in Georgia and ends in Maine. Thousands of people attempt to accomplish this goal in one trip every year but only about one in four finish it, but Brad did it. He walked every day for four and a half months to accomplish this one goal. Brad is a very goal-oriented person. When he wants to do something, he starts taking the steps in the direction of his goal. Each step he takes is intentional and consistent, be it big or small, to get him closer to what he is trying to do. He made a very simple statement one day in church but when implemented in our lives, can change the whole trajectory of it. He was talking about goals. He said, "If you want to accomplish something big, you have to make small consistent choices. Small consistent choices over time create big results."

How did he walk the entire Appalachian Trail? He took small steps every day. He didn't just start in Georgia then magically appear in Maine. It took consistent daily decisions to make the next steps for this to happen. This principle is true in everything. If you want to lose weight you have to make the small decisions at every meal to eat good food instead of bad food. If you want to write a book you have to buy an alarm clock and get up every day, drink large amounts of iced coffee (maybe that's just me), and write small sections of words that will eventually add up to a book. If you want to get into shape you have to make the daily decision to work out and not sit on the couch. If you want to take a road trip you have to get in your car and drive each mile. If you want there to be peace and trust in your marriage you must get up every day and make those consistent small decisions that will add up over time and build that peace and trust in your relationship.

So, if this is so simple and will create so much change why is it so hard to do?! Well for one reason we're lazy. Let me speak some real words right now. We all want the big results, but we don't want to make the small consistent steps. We want the hot body, the written book, the adventure, and the great marriage to happen without doing anything to make it happen. We want instant gratification without any effort on our behalf. We live in a microwave, text message, and prime world. If you want to communicate with someone on the other side of the planet, they can have your message in seconds. You can order basically anything on Amazon Prime and have it in 2 days or less. In fact, I heard yesterday that Amazon is changing it to 1-day shipping, what a time to be alive! We really don't have to wait on much anymore. Now, don't get me wrong, I love the convenience this allows me. I am all about not waiting and the fact that Walmart will do my grocery shopping for me makes me happy on a level I can't even put into words. There is nothing wrong with these conveniences, but there is something wrong with the mindset these conveniences have created.

We have grown totally impatient. We don't want things to develop, we want things to happen instantly. We have this mindset things will just happen without any effort and we don't want to take the time to build or establish anything. The world has led us to believe things should just happen and if they don't then we should walk away and find something that will. But here's the deal, things do not just happen. Walking the Appalachian Trail does not just happen. Achieving goals does not just happen. Good marriages do not just happen. Peace and trust in a marriage do not just happen. It must be built over time by making those small consistent choices. In most situations, we only see the end goal. Alex and I didn't walk the Appalachian trail with Brad. We saw him accomplish the goal through pictures on social media, but we didn't see the blood, sweat, frustration, determination, and tears it took to accomplish this goal. We didn't see the days he wanted to quit but made the choice to keep going. All we saw was that he finished. When all we see is the end result, we tend to believe it was easy and natural, that it just happened effortlessly. But it didn't just happen. Brad had to get up every day and make a consistent decision to keep going. We must do the same thing in our marriages. There will be hard days. There will be days that you want to quit. There will be days you have to work at it. Every couple you know, that is happy now, is only happy now because at some point they decided not to give up. Nothing just happens, it takes work. Nothing worth having just comes naturally and smoothly all the time.

Every mile gets us further down the road on our adventure and every choice we make to pour into our marriages will build them up and draw us closer together as a couple. Marriage is not something you arrive at and never have to do work again. It's not something that is delivered in 2 days. It's something you work at your entire life.

I recently read an article in a magazine where two famous movie stars had been interviewed. The whole article was about their marriage and how they had stayed together through some very rough seasons. I read it because I wanted to know how they were going to represent marriage. The world, through the movie industry, tells us it should be easy, and if it isn't, something is wrong, and we have married the wrong person. Throughout the whole article, the two actors talked about how they had to decide to stay together. The article ended with these two quotes, "Anything you have to work at, the outcome is always more rewarding. We had to work really hard at being a couple because we're both incredibly, painfully stubborn." and "All these movies taught us about love at first sight and that it's supposed to be easy. It took me a while to realize that was such a lie, because the things you work really, really hard for always yield the best results."

As I read that last sentence I thought, "Yes, this couple gets it." They understand it's a process. They understand it takes work, but it's worth it. They understand that neither one of them is perfect, but that's ok, it just means they must work harder. They understand those small consistent choices over time create big results. And that is what I want you to understand through this chapter and this book. You can have a peaceful marriage full of trust, but you must do the work. Your spouse doesn't have to be perfect; you don't have to be perfect, and your situation doesn't have to be perfect, you just have to be consistent. If you do this, if you make the decision not to give up and you make those daily choices to make your marriage better, you will get the results you are looking for. So, let's talk about some practical choices we can make consistently to start gaining that peace and trust.

Practical Consistent Decisions

- Be Honest

If we are going to have peace and trust in our marriages, we always have to start by being completely honest with our spouses. A good marriage can't be built on a foundation of lies. Eventually, the lies will cause the relationship to crumble. It's so easy to think a little white lie won't hurt anything. Deep down we all want to believe that, but the problem with lying is you never get to stop. One lie leads to another lie, which leads to another lie. The situation continues to grow bigger and bigger to cover for all the lies that were told, but at the root of it was one little white lie. Most major problem can be traced back to one little white lie. In the last chapter, I talked about how affairs start with an innocent conversation. No one just wakes up and decides it's a good day to have an affair. The same is true with major lies. No one just wakes up one day and tells this major, complicated lie to ruin their marriage. It all starts with the choice to make the first small one and it builds from there until one day you realize your marriage is in shambles because of all the lies that have been told. With the presence of lies comes suspicion, and when you have suspicion in your relationship peace and trust are out the door.

I want to give you a light-hearted example of how serious lying is in your marriage. I say light heart only because when you read this you are probably going to be like, really this is your example?!?! Yes, it's simple and silly, but the Lord has used this small example to teach me how lies can affect a marriage.

Alex and I are very truthful with each other. We always

communicated about any plans we have or any purchases that have been made. Alex has full access to my computer and phone, and I have the same access to his. We know each other's passwords and login ins. At any point, we could pick up the other one's phone and look through it. We have nothing in there to hide from each other, so we don't care if the other one looks at it. We don't hide anything from each other until Christmas and birthdays roll around. That's the only time we will tell each other not to look at our email, phones, or computers. That's the only time we hide anything from each other.

Now before you jump to conclusions about what I'm going to say just hang in there with me. Keeping these secrets is fine. I'm not saying it's wrong to keep those kinds of secrets. It's so we can surprise each other, but can I share something with you. There is a lack of peace even in those innocent moments of secrecy. Even in the moments, when I'm keeping a secret from Alex because of a gift I'm giving him, there is a lack of peace. I'm constantly worried that he will find out what it is. I'm constantly trying to keep it a secret because I want him to be surprised when the special day comes around. So, if keeping a good secret creates a lack of peace, how much more damage does keeping a bad one cause?

At this exact moment, I am dealing with that lack of peace. Alex's birthday is coming up soon and I have gotten him the gift to end all gifts, but I must keep it a secret until the day comes. This particular gift has required a lot of secrets for it to be presented to him correctly. I can't wait for the big day! I'm exhausted from keeping it from him. This gift is so big I've had to include other people in it to help me with it. So not only do I have to not let anything slip, but I must make sure they don't say anything by accident. I must make sure he doesn't see the emails about the gift. I had to tell him not to check the mail because I had ordered things. I'm having to watch my words more carefully. Just yesterday I opened my mouth and almost said something that would have totally given it away. Again, this is all over a gift I'm giving him. In this case, I'm not lying to cover up something bad. I'm just not telling him the details of a good thing I am doing for him. However, the effects are similar. I'm not experiencing the peace I usually have because of this gift.

Through this example, the Lord has taught me a valuable lesson. Keeping secrets in a marriage not only hurts the marriage, but it also negatively affects you. I feel nervous he will find out what his gift is, but how much more nervous would I be if I was telling a lie that was bad and could possibly ruin our marriage? It would cause me to act differently which would cause situations to arise in our marriage that weren't necessary or helpful. Honestly, I don't see how people function when they are keeping negative things from their spouses. They are really making life so much harder than it has to be. I can't think of anything on this planet that would be worth living in that constant state of anxiety and tension. They are choosing to walk on this adventure and make things harder instead of using the keys, and to me, it's just not worth the lack of peace.

At the end of the day, it's so much easier to just tell the truth and go about your day. I once heard someone say, "Tell the truth that way you don't have to remember anything." Isn't that so true? When we tell the truth, we can go about our normal lives knowing we won't slip up. Peace and trust are more valuable than we give them credit for. Don't lose them over a little white lie. It may seem small and insignificant, but a little lie will grow into something much bigger. Save yourself a lot of trouble and just be honest.

- Keep Your Word

Have you ever told your spouse that you would do something and then not do it for whatever reason? Yeh, I have too. Life happens and we get busy and sometimes things fall through the cracks. This particular way of building trust is easy and yet hard at the same time. The good thing about this one is when we stay true to our word with the little things, over time it will help to establish trust in our marriage.

Your marriage will probably not fall apart if you forget to take out the trash; however, by doing what you say you will do, it will develop a level of trust that can help strengthen your marriage. It can keep those little arguments from happening which will lead to greater peace. I think we take for granted how much the little things add up over time in both positive and negative ways. If you're constantly shown your spouse can be trusted with the little things, you can trust them in all things whereas when the little things are constantly not happening, you tend to not trust them at all with the bigger things.

Little things left undone over time leads to resentment which leads to passive-aggressive comments which lead to a lack of peace. Have you ever been around a couple that just bickers all the time? As you are reading this you probably have a couple that comes to mind or maybe you are that couple. Being around that constant tension isn't a very fun place to be. I know a couple like that, and I don't enjoy being with them when they're together because I know all they're going to do is be snappy at each other the whole time. I personally never want to be the couple other people don't want to be around. I want mine and Alex's relationship to be life-giving, not life-draining. One way you avoid becoming that couple is by doing what you say you will do. I haven't done any studies on the matter, but I bet if we looked back into the lives of the couples that seem to constantly stay annoyed with each other, the problem could probably be traced back to lack of trust and peace that developed from things falling through the cracks on a regular basis. Little things over time add up. It can start as simply as being annoyed about the trash not being taken out until one day you are the couple that no one wants to be around.

Keeping your word over time will add up one way or the other. By keeping your word over time trust and peace will thrive. Now be encouraged, we're not all perfect all the time. I get that! Remember I started this section by admitting I've told Alex that I would do things and then not follow through on it. Here's the deal with this, consistency adds up, so when you do have those moments, when you forget to do something, they won't affect your marriage as badly because of all the times you did come through. Just let the positives outweigh the negatives. You don't have to be perfect just do your best! Keep your word!

- Keep Your Family's Best Interests at Heart

Finally, if you're going to build trust and peace in your marriages, you must be present by having frequent conversations with your spouses and make good decisions based on whatever situations arise in your relationship. You need to make decisions that are best for your marriage and your family. You need to be wise with the resources you have and the blessings you have been given. One-way Alex has built peace and trust with me is by being a hard worker and providing for me. I get that Alex doesn't want to go to work most days. I don't want to go to work most days; however, not only does he get up every day and go to work, but he gives it his 100% effort, so he brings home a good paycheck every week. This gives me a great deal of peace. Because of the decisions Alex makes we will have the resources we need for the things we need.

I also know Alex isn't going to blow all the money he makes either. We pay tithe, pay our bills, save, and get our necessities first before we spend money on ourselves. Alex and I actually don't spend a lot of money without talking to each other about it. It's just a habit we have gotten into, but it has helped us out a great deal by both of us knowing where our money is going. You may be reading this and think this is a no brainer but there are people who don't make those good decisions. There are people who refuse to work and provide for their families. There are people who go to work but then use the money on things other than their family's needs. This kind of lifestyle will not be conducive for peace and trust. By being present, having conversations, and making wise decisions you are creating an atmosphere where peace and trust will not only grow, but will thrive.

In that spirit of peace and trust, your relationship will continue to grow deeper and stronger. When you have that peace and trust established you may not have to have as many conversations because you know the other person will make the right decisions, what a wonderful feeling, knowing that your spouse has your best interest at heart and will make decisions based off that.

Start at the Bottom, and Build Again

Continually pursue peace with everyone
HEBREWS 12:14 AMPLIFIED VERSION (EMPHASIS MINE)

So, at this point, I hope you understand how important peace and trust are in a marriage and how possessing them can make your adventure so much smoother and more enjoyable. But what do we do if that peace and trust have been broken? Maybe it has been broken through small decisions over a period of time or maybe it was a very bad mistake. Regardless of the circumstances surrounding the break, the way to rebuild is the same. Start at the bottom and build again.

- Clear the Broken Pieces

What happens when a structure collapses? You go in, clean up the broken pieces, and start fresh with new material. The same is true in our marriages. If peace and trust have been broken, the first thing we must do is clear the broken pieces. We must genuinely want to change the situation and ask for forgiveness. Depending on what happened this step can happen quickly, or it may take time, but forgiveness and clearing the broken pieces is the first step. We must acknowledge the break happened. We must clear the ground for the new material to come in. Asking for forgiveness can be hard, but the rebuild can't take place on top of the rubble. If we try to rebuild on broken pieces the rebuild won't be secured and will collapse again when the smallest issue arises. So, take the time to do the cleanup first before you start the rebuild.

- Rebuild Your Foundation

After you have cleared everything by apologizing then the real work begins- the rebuild. You must start with a foundation of small consistent choices and work your way up from there. You must make those daily consistent decisions that will re-establish peace and trust. The foundation of a structure is the most important part. If we don't take the time to establish a strong foundation anything that comes at us can cause major problems in our marriages. In Matthew 7:24-27, we find the story of the wise man who built his house on a strong foundation and the foolish man who built his house on the sand. Because the wise man built his house on the rock, when the storms of life came, his house remained strong. But the foolish man built his house on the sand, and when the storm came, he wasn't as lucky. In the Amplified Bible, it says "great and complete was its fall". This man lost everything because of a bad foundation, everything. One bad choice of not having a strong foundation led to complete destruction for this man. That is what's happening in marriages today. We aren't establishing the correct foundation and because of that, the storms of life are causing our relationships to collapse. Let's take the time to build that foundation correctly. It will take work, but it will be worth the work in the long run. In fact, if we have a strong foundation it will save us from having certain problems down the road.

- Continue to Build Upon that Foundation

If restoration is what you want, and I so hope it is, it will take work, but please don't give up. The process of rebuilding a foundation will take at least double the effort it would have before the break, maybe even more. Even if forgiveness has been extended and received, it's hard to forget things sometimes. Once suspicion and doubt enter a relationship, it will take time to remove them, but over time if you are consistent you will see the foundation of peace and trust begin to take shape again. You will see suspicion and doubt start to fade away.

It may be hard. It may seem like nothing is happening for a while. Be patient. Put in the work. Use your keys. Do whatever it takes to rebuild your marriage! Peace and trust will start to take shape and replace the suspicion and doubt in your marriage, and it will be worth every moment of hard work to have these two things restored in your relationship. As you make those daily decisions you will start to see a change in your marriage. As you build on that strong foundation your marriage will begin to grow tall and strong. With every consistent decision, the bond between you and your spouse will grow stronger.

Before we leave this section, a word of advice for the one that had their peace and trust broken by their spouse. If they have asked for forgiveness and are beginning the rebuilding process, please don't make it harder for them than it has to be. Yes, I know it hurts, maybe more than I could ever imagine. Yes, maybe they were totally wrong for doing what they did. But if they have come to you truly repentant, use this opportunity to model the love of Jesus. Extend grace, praise the progress, however slow it may seem. Don't get historical and constantly bring the offense back up. If you have forgiven them, act like it. Get down and help them rebuild. Jesus not only forgives us, but He gets down in our mess with us and help us out of it. Let's do this with our spouses. Let's be a part of the rebuild. Just imagine the new heights your marriage will achieve when you are both working together.

Work Smarter Not Harder

We have been given the keys that will make this adventure smooth. They have literally already been given to us as a gift. We just have to use them. Why make the decision to walk when you have the keys to ride? Storms of life will come, bumps in the road will happen, there will be hard days, but don't make things harder than they have to be by inconsistency, lies, and selfishness. Be consistent, be honest, do your best, use your keys, it will make the adventure so much easier and so much more enjoyable! Remember small consistent decisions over time lead to big results. You can do this, make good decisions and don't give up!

PART 3

TRAVEL WELL TOGETHER

CHAPTER 8

EXPLORE THE AREA (COMPROMISE)

Compromise is not about losing. It is about deciding that
the other person has just as much right to be
happy with the end result as you do
~ Donna Martini

What is one thing that makes going on an adventure so much fun? As I was pondering this question several answers came to mind. One, you're getting out of your usual routine. You're leaving the 9-5 of normal life and getting a chance to relax and have fun. You're seeing new things, eating new food, and enjoying new experiences. You're getting the chance to explore life in a new setting with a new point of view. You get to see how others live for a few days and what normal looks like to them. You get to see the beauty of this world. There are a lot of reasons why people enjoy adventures, but one of my favorite reasons is I get to explore all the things that the Lord has created. I get to search out the beauty of God's workmanship. I tell people all the time, I want to go to all the places, and I want to see all the things. I want to explore everything. I want to see and learn all I can about the world that I live in. All adventures should have some kind of exploration to them if they are going to be true adventures. I mean, who goes out of town just to do the same things that they can do in town? One way, Alex and I explore when we go on adventures is by not doing anything we could do at home. That means we must explore the area to see what it offers. That means we must get out of the hotel room and see the sights. Exploring makes our adventures more fun and because of it, we get to fully experience the adventure. My prayer for all of our trips is, *"Abba, show us wild and beautiful things. Meet us there and speak to us in ways that only we will understand."* The beautiful thing is, He always does and because of that we always grow closer to Him, and because we experience it together, we grow closer to each other as well. Exploring not only makes the adventure better, it makes us better.

So, what does exploring have to do with marriage? As I was preparing to write this book on marriage being a beautiful adventure, I started a list of words I felt applied in our marriages. After I had listed all the words I could think of, I wanted to reach out to others and see what they had to say about what it took to have a happy marriage. I'm not naive enough to think that Alex and I have all the answers when it comes to marriage, so I started really studying, praying, and reaching out to other couples I knew were thriving in their relationships. Everyone gave me the words that instantly pop into everyone's head when you think of marriage like faithfulness and honesty, but there was one word that kept coming up repeatedly. No matter who I ask, young, old, newly married or married for years, this one word kept coming up as something that had to happen if you were going to have a marriage that was a beautiful adventure. That word was "compromise".

According to Google~ One of the definitions of compromise is- *"an agreement or a settlement of a dispute that is reached by each side making concessions."* A compromise happens when there are at least two people that have a difference in opinion on how a situation should be handled. In order for a compromise to happen both parties must make the decision to give a little. Neither side completely gets their way in the matter when a compromise is reached, but they agree upon the terms. When a couple compromises, they are choosing to say there isn't a right side and a wrong side, but an agreed upon decision. Then they go forward with the decision they made.

As I was thinking about the word compromise, and how it's necessary for a marriage to work, the word explore came to mind as well. So, in my true nerd form, I looked up the definition for the word explore. According to Google~ the word explore means- *"travel in or through in order to learn about or familiarize oneself with it, inquire into or discuss (a subject or issue) in detail, or examine or evaluate (an option or possibility)."* When I looked at the definitions to both words, I see how they could be used interchangeably in marriage. We are traveling through this adventure of marriage together and through it, we are constantly learning more about how our spouse views and responses to situations. When we take the time to discuss issues in detail and explore other options, possibilities, and points of view by having an open mind compromise happens. Compromising with our spouse is a way of exploring all the possibilities. Through compromise, we can see things from different perspectives, and if we're willing, we will learn that there is more than one correct way to do things.

It Doesn't Come Naturally

Compromise must happen a lot in marriages if they are going to be happy. I one hundred percent believe that is true, but can I just be transparent for a moment and say I don't like compromising? It's not something that just comes naturally to me, and if you're honest, I'm sure you would say the same thing about yourself. I mean, genuinely, who enjoys not getting their way? Unfortunately, it coming naturally to me doesn't dictate whether or not I should practice it. Somethings are easier to compromise on than others, but in general, compromise is not fun, but fun or not it's necessary, and also helpful, to our relationship when it's practiced regularly. Compromise must be something we do because it is necessary, not because it comes naturally. We can't dig our heels into the sand and be stubborn about everything and expect this adventure to go smoothly. We can't be selfish and force people to always do things our way and expect a healthy relationship with our spouses. We can't be naive enough to believe our way is the only correct way. We must be willing to explore the possibility there are other, and dare I say even better ways, to handle situations than the way we want to handle them. We must be willing to allow our spouse to have input and be a part of the decision making in our marriages and our families. We are on this adventure as a team, and if we're going to arrive happily at our destination, exploring different routes through compromise is a must. We are going to use this chapter to discuss what we can learn about compromise from Jesus's life, how we can implement compromise into our daily routine, and examples of how other couples are putting compromise into action in their marriages, and how we can benefit from their wisdom. Let's start exploring!

Exploration: Did Jesus Compromise?

Therefore become imitators of God [copy Him and follow His example], as well-beloved children [imitate their father]; and walk continually in love [that is, value one another—practice empathy and compassion, unselfishly seeking the best for others], just as Christ also loved you and gave Himself up for us, an offering and sacrifice to God [slain for you, so that it became] a sweet fragrance

EPHESIANS 5:1 AMPLIFIED VERSION

When every couple, without fail, mentioned compromise as being an imperative part of marriage, I decided to study and figure out why it was so important. As I was studying, I ran across this verse in Ephesians. Although the word compromise wasn't used directly it got my wheels turning. If we're supposed to be imitators of Jesus, the first thing we need to do is to find out what Jesus was like. You can't imitate someone if you don't know anything about them. Then that led me to another thought. Did Jesus ever compromise? So, I started looking at the New Testament to see if I saw any evidence that He did.

When we read the New Testament, we learn a lot about the character of Jesus and how He lived His life. Jesus was passionate about the Father and doing the work He was commissioned to accomplish; however, everything He did was from a stance of love and compassion. Jesus loved people. Nowhere in the Bible do you see Jesus pushing His agenda on anyone in a forceful way. He simply taught the crowd and then left the outcome to them. He wasn't domineering at all. He spoke truth in a loving way. He was empathetic to everyone He met. Although He was the Son of God with all authority, He never used that authority like a dictatorship with His people. He was a shepherd that guided His flock. Although He was the Son of God, He never ran away from someone challenging His word or became defensive when people questioned Him. In fact, it seemed like He enjoyed when people challenged Him. Some of my favorite moments in the New Testament are when the Pharisees questioned Jesus. He always rose to the occasion and never backed down from them, yet His answers were always intended to draw them to God, not just to make them look like idiots. Although, typically with them, the latter was always what ended up happening. These moments when questions arose gave Him a platform to speak more in-depth about the Father and why He was here, in hopes that people would accept Him as Savior. Let's look at an example of how Jesus handled being questioned in John chapter 3.

In this chapter, a Pharisee, Nicodemus, has come to Jesus at night because he wants to talk to Him. Now right off the bat Jesus could have been upset with Nicodemus because he chose to come to Him in secret instead of addressing Him in public with his questions, but we don't see even a hint of frustration on Jesus' part. In fact, Nicodemus spends the entire conversation, or at least the part of the conversation that is documented, questioning Jesus. Jesus answers every single question Nicodemus throws at Him. As I read this chapter, I don't see Jesus as being irritated or frustrated with Nicodemus. I see Him very calm and patient yet speaking truth. He tells Nicodemus that as a Pharisee he should already know some of these things, but He goes on to explain them anyway. Again, there is that truth seasoned in love. He doesn't condemn Nicodemus but spurs him on to be better. He doesn't shut Nicodemus down either, He lets him voice all his doubts on the subject without interruption before He addresses each one. It was a two-way conversation the entire time with both people being able to communicate fully. Not one person running over the other and pushing their point of view. So, with this story running in my head, the Lord brought these verses to mind.

> *Have this same attitude in yourselves which was in Christ Jesus [look to Him as your example in selfless humility], who, although He existed in the form and unchanging essence of God [as One with Him, possessing the fullness of all the divine attributes—the entire nature of deity], did not regard equality with God a thing to be grasped or asserted [as if He did not already possess it, or was afraid of losing it]; but emptied Himself [without renouncing or diminishing His deity, but only temporarily giving up the outward expression of divine equality and His rightful dignity] by assuming the form of a bond-servant, and being made in the likeness of men [He became completely human but was without sin, being fully God and fully man].*
>
> *PHILIPPIANS 2:5-7 AMPLIFIED VERSION*

If there was ever someone that didn't have to compromise it was Jesus. He didn't have to come down to earth to die on a cross because of our sins. But He did. When He was on earth, He didn't have to treat us as His children. But He did. He didn't have to answer questions and address the concerns of the people that came to Him. But He did. He could have come down and asserted His full power and treated us as servants and it would have been completely fair, but He didn't come in that manner. He came as a friend, not a master. He came to draw our hearts closer to the Father. Did Jesus compromise? Yes, I think He did, and I believe He did it in the wildest and most beautiful way.

I looked a little deeper into the many definitions of compromise and there was another definition that caught my attention. Compromise also means to *accept lower standards.* I believe this is the way Jesus compromised for us. He humbled Himself. He stepped down from His position in Heaven and took on all our human qualities so He could carry out the plan for our salvation. He compromised His authority, temporarily, with the end goal being our ability to spend eternity with Him. Although He was fully God, He also became fully man for us. He came down to our level so He could ultimately lift us up to His level. He could have come down in the fullness of His position and authority. He could have been domineering, but He wasn't. He compromised for us. He came as a shepherd, not a dictator. He came as a Father, not a ruler. And we are told in both Ephesians 5 and Philippians 2 to be like Jesus. We need to compromise in order to have a beautiful adventure. We need to compromise in order to be more like Jesus. Compromise is not a bad thing. Hearing people out is not a bad thing. Humbling ourselves is not a bad thing. It's a beautiful thing Jesus has demonstrated for us in the most amazing way. Compromising didn't diminish the fact that Jesus was the Son of God in one bit. He was fully God and fully man. By compromising, Jesus made a way for us to be with Him, and through compromise we can make our marriages better every single day.

You may not see what Jesus did as being a compromise; but think about His position versus how He handles us as a Father. He possesses all authority, all leadership, all dominion. He doesn't need our help in any way. Yet He comes to us as a Father, a Shepherd, and a Friend. He calls us into fellowship and partnership with Him to further His Kingdom. I believe this is where we can be imitators of Jesus in our marriage. We can choose to come alongside our spouse and partner with them in making decisions. We can choose to communicate with our spouses by not being domineering and shutting them down whenever their concerns and opinions differ from our own. We can choose to be gentle in how we handle our spouses instead of forceful and defensive. We can choose to be like Jesus and compromise in the most wild and beautiful way, and by doing so strengthen our marriage. Accepting lower standards has such a negative feel to it, but it doesn't have to be negative. Jesus came down to earth for us, but the above verse also says He never sinned. So, although He compromised His position, He didn't compromise His Lordship. We need to be like Jesus, and compromise for the ultimate good of our marriage. That might mean being quiet and fully listening before we speak. That might mean doing things in a completely different way than we want too. I'm so glad Jesus compromised His position for my salvation and my goodness, I want (and need) to be more like Jesus, in life and in my marriage.

How do we do this? How do we explore compromise in our marriages? Like I said earlier, compromise isn't a natural response for any of us. Compromise is a decision we must make every day whenever a situation arises where we do not see eye to eye. It's something that must be intentionally explored. It's one thing to talk about compromise, it's a whole other monster when you actually have to do it. So, let's look at some practical things you can do to implement compromise into your daily life with your spouse.

Applying Compromise

- Explore Different Routes to Your Destination

Did you know there are about 7 different ways to get to the Grand Canyon from Alabama? I didn't know this until about 2 years ago. When we decided to go there for Alex's birthday, he sat down and mapped out all the possible ways we could go. Each route would get us to the same destination. Some were longer and more scenic. Some were quicker and easier. There were also multiple forms of transportation we could take as well. We could fly, drive, or take a train, but at the end of the day we would end up at the Grand Canyon. Alex mapped out all the different routes, then he sat down with me and let me help decide which way to go. As I think back on this moment, Alex was demonstrating compromise in marriage so perfectly here. He had explored all possibilities. He had done all the homework. He could have just picked the first route Google maps suggested and stopped there. What is wild to me is what he did next. He brought all the options to me and let me help pick the route. In this case, he was the one that had studied everything out. He had the power just to pick the way and we go. Had he done that it would have been totally fine because he was the driver and he had put in the research time, but that wasn't how he handled it. He involved me in the decision and planning process. We worked together to pick the best path for our adventure.

Just like there were multiple routes to get to the Grand Canyon; there are multiple ways to achieve your goals. There is always more than just one right way. We must be open to the idea that there are multiple ways to arrive at our destination. We must be open to the idea that there may be ways that are better than ours to get us there. We must be willing to work together as a team to make this adventure work. The main goal here is to be opened minded. When your spouse comes to you with another option hear them out. Listen to what they have to say and be open to the idea that their way may be better. Work as a team and discuss all the options. It may be that both ideas could use some adjustment and a compromise can be found. The beautiful thing is, if we're intentional about these moments of disagreement, they don't have to turn into moments of discord. Just because you disagree doesn't mean you have to argue. These moments can become moments of growth and unity if we communicate with open minds instead of shooting each down. If we will keep the end goal in mind instead of the winner/loser mentality, we will be able to compromise a lot easier and achieve our goals a lot quicker.

There have been moments when Alex and I have gotten this right and there have been times that we have gotten it so wrong. There have been moments when we walk away from a conversation frustrated because one or both of us feel like the other one did not hear us out. Those times never feel good. It's so easy to take it personally when your spouse doesn't think your idea or opinion is a good one. It's the idea or opinion that was disagreed upon, but it's so easy to take it as a personal attack. That's why it is so important to be open-minded and communicate through the disagreement and find some common ground. The moments we get it right feel so good. When we walk away from a decision knowing we have been heard and valued it makes all the difference. That is where compromise comes in- taking the time to listen and be open-minded goes such a long way. We are a work in progress just like everyone else, but by being open-minded and exploring compromise we have grown, and I have seen such a difference in both of us. Every time we get it right, we draw closer together and when we get it wrong, it's a lesson learned. There is never a clear-cut winner or loser. When it comes to communication and compromise, we either win together or we lose together.

- Ok, Pause, Question

If we're going to get better at compromising, we must find practical ways to walk it out in our everyday lives. I mentioned earlier, we all like to get our way and we don't like to compromise. Taking the time to view different routes to our destinations will take intentionality. It's not going to just happen on its own. Our natural response will always be to do things our way based on our perspective. We will have to train ourselves to take a moment to step back and view things differently. The best way I have found to do that is by pausing and asking questions. How do we get a better view of something we are physically looking at? We step back so we can see the whole thing and then we stand still to take it all in. Then if we can we ask questions about it. We can do the same in our communication with our spouses. When they present a different way to do things instead of instantly going into how it's wrong and your way is better, pause. Before you respond really think about what they just said. Entertain the idea that what they said could work. After you have given it some thought, if it still doesn't make sense, ask questions. You will be amazed at how much you can learn by simply asking them to explain their idea a little more instead of instantly shooting their idea down.

Alex and I haven't always communicated very well especially during moments when we didn't see eye to eye. We both have strong personalities and there are certain things that we both want done in certain ways. We were both guilty of instantly shooting down the other one's ideas as soon as it was spoken. That only led to unnecessary arguments and feelings getting hurt. We started implementing the "ok, pause, question" method to our communication, and it has helped us so much when it comes to compromising and honestly just talking in general.

Alex started using it during arguments to help us communicate better. Alex processes things quicker than I do so it was easy for him to dominate an argument, so he started pausing to give me time to process and then respond. This worked great for me. In fact, it worked so well that now we use it a lot in our decision making and daily conversations, not just arguments. It's simple. Whenever one of us presences a possible action or solution, the other one says, "ok" then we pause. We acknowledge we heard what was said, but we don't say anything else for a moment or two. We really think about what we just heard. We really try to understand what they said and if it will work to accomplish whatever our goal is. If it will work, we go forward with it. If we don't completely understand how it would work, we ask questions. I personally love this way of compromising by using this method because I feel heard and I feel like I am a part of the team.

Alex is a fixer. Like I said before, he is very quick on his feet and a fast processor. When there is a problem or a decision to be made Alex has about 5 possible solutions bouncing in his head in seconds. If he isn't intentional about pausing, he can have the whole matter planned out on his own before I have processed what the actual problem is. When he pauses after I have said something, I feel like he is really listening to me instead of just brushing me off or problem solving. Since I feel heard and acknowledged, I don't mind if he questions me about it. This gives me the opportunity to explain my point of view even more. This also gives Alex a platform to explain the reasons why he is questioning it and explain his point of view as well. There have been times we have gone completely with his way or completely with my way, but typically from these conversations, we settled on a compromise. We each contribute to what the solution should be.

Alex and I have become way better at compromising by simply taking the time to pause and really consider the other person's point of view. A lot of the arguments and problems can be avoided altogether if your spouse feels like you are listening to them, acknowledging them, and including them in the process. So, the next time you and your spouse don't see eye to eye, just pause. Let them know you are listening, and you do value their input. Make them feel like an important part of the team. Then ask questions and talk through all the possibilities instead of instantly telling them all the ways they're wrong. This one thing can completely change the way you and your spouse communicate, and compromise will start to come more naturally.

- Don't View Questions as an Attack

We learned above that Jesus never got upset when people questioned Him, in fact, He always used it to His advantage to further His mission. A lot of growth can happen in marriage if we will model this when compromise needs to happen. When you implement the "ok, pause, question" method, you have to allow for the questions. You can't get defensive when your spouse is questioning your idea or point of view. If you do, it will not bring the compromise you desire. View these questions as your spouse getting the information they need, instead of them shutting you down. Stay calm and seize the opportunity to really communicate why you think it would be a good idea to go with your plan. Through those questions, your spouse may realize it's a good idea, or you may realize it isn't, but regardless of the outcome, you have communicated through something instead of arguing. Compromise isn't about one being right and the other being wrong. It's about two people working together as a team to achieve a desired outcome. There are no winners or losers in marriage. That should never be our end goal. Remember in marriage you win as a team or lose as a team. The goal should always be harmony in your relationship and an outcome you're both happy with, not a clear winner or loser.

Compromise in Action

There are so many areas in a marriage where compromise must happen. Each couple has their own areas based upon their lifestyle and their family dynamic. I didn't want to leave this subject without giving some real-life examples of compromise in action. Remember,

I said every couple I talked to said compromise was important? So, I went back to them after I started writing this chapter and asked them to give me examples of how they put compromise into action in their marriages. I did this for two reasons. First, I wanted some practical examples so I would know how these couples were walking this out. Second, although each couple is different and will have to compromise differently, I felt like some examples may help to give you a starting point in your own marriage. Compromise, just like exploring, is active. It takes intentional decisions and daily conversations. It takes trial and error. When it comes to compromising in our marriage, we have got to work it, for it to work for us. Things will not just fall into place without any effort on our part. We must explore and seek it out. Don't give up on it. Compromise can be developed over time. The more we put it into practice, the better we will get at it. Let's look at some real-life examples of compromise in action.

- Work Compromise

One of the couples I spoke with had to do a lot of compromising when it came to starting their own business. They knew, without a shadow of a doubt, the Lord was calling the wife into starting her own business. However, even though it was from the Lord, they still had to do a lot of compromising for their marriage not to be affected negatively, because of the changes it would bring. Starting this business meant losing some income in the beginning, it meant losing time with each other, family, and friends. It meant going into debt to get it off the ground. All those things could have had a negative impact on their relationship had they been left uncommunicated. They sat down and discussed all the changes the business would bring. Once they agreed upon everything, they started executing the plan. The business is growing, and their relationship is thriving because this couple took the time to make the decisions together and explore compromise.

148

- Travel Compromise

Another couple who told me compromise was important for marriage has recently had to explore compromise in a new area. They recently had their first baby. They both love to travel; however, it's difficult to do that when you have a new baby in the house, so they haven't been able to travel much. It has been a little over a year since they had their baby and the husband is ready to start taking little getaways with just him and his wife. The wife isn't ready to leave the baby overnight yet. Instead of this becoming a huge point of disagreement for them, they compromised on taking day trips until the wife was ready to leave the baby overnight. They both honored each other's desires in this situation instead of it becoming a strain on their marriage.

- Holiday Compromise

Yet another couple told me how holidays were a time for compromise for them. When they came into their relationship, they both had traditions with their families they wanted to continue to honor. However, you can't be all the places, all the time, and they were starting their own family and wanted to start new traditions of their own. They explore compromise by sitting down and really planning out their holidays in order to make all the traditions they wanted to do a priority. They chose to work together on how and where they are going to spend their time during the holidays. As they were sharing this with me, I was reminded of several couples that struggle during the holiday season. By simply sitting down and compromising during this time there doesn't have to be a struggle at all. You can actually enjoy the holiday season by just doing a little preplanning and compromising.

- Home Decor Compromise

One wife told me she had to learn to compromise on the home they lived in and how it was decorated. Her husband wanted to be a part of all those details. He wanted a say in the house they bought, where it was located, and how it was decorated. She shared with me how, at first, she thought it was a little strange that he wanted to be a part of those things, especially the decorating. She had to learn his opinion mattered and he lived there also, so he should have a say in things. They are both strong willed people. They had to learn to work together as a team in this area. They had to allow for both voices to be heard and be a part of those decisions with their home. They made compromises, so both people could be happy with the space they live in.

Start Today

Little children (believers, dear ones), let us not love [merely in theory] with word or with tongue [giving lip service to compassion], but in action and in truth [in practice and in sincerity, because practical acts of love are more than words].
1 JOHN 3:18 AMPLIFIED VERSION

Those are just a few examples of how couples are putting compromise into action to make their adventures a little smoother. I hope those examples get your wheels turning on how compromise can be explored in your own relationship. Every couple is different, which means your compromise may look different than others. That's totally fine, the point isn't to compromise like someone else, but to gain wisdom from them in a way that grows your marriage. We can learn so much from other couples.

So much of how we act and the decisions we make is based on our perspective. Our temperaments, and our past experiences also factor into our decision making and behavior. When you put two people together, they tend to see things two different ways. Even though we're looking at the exact same thing, both people will notice things the other one completely missed. I believe the Lord created us that way so when we communicate and work together as a team, we can get the whole picture. It would be foolish of us not to use all our resources and reach out to other couples that are compromising well. By being opened mind to your spouse and getting wisdom from other couples, compromise can start happening in your own marriage.

1 John 3:18 tells us love should be put into action if it is going to be fully received. I believe one way to put love into action is by compromise. When we chose to explore our spouse's point of view, we are showing them we love and value them. We are showing them their opinion matters to us. Practical acts of love through compromise speak volumes to our spouses and in turn, can change our marriages for the better. Actions do speak louder than words, so it's important that once a compromise has been agreed upon, both parties walk it out. Don't bring further hurt and disagreement into your marriage by saying one thing and doing another. Compromise is important, but it must be communicated and then honored if it's going to give you the outcome you desire.

Maybe you are already exploring compromise in your marriage, if so, that is great and please continue to do so! Maybe you haven't compromised at all and you are feeling the effects of that right now. My encouragement to you is to start today! Start exploring your spouse's ideas, opinions, and their point of view. Be open-minded to different routes to your desired destination and find a way to compromise, so you are both happy with the decisions being made. Take some time today to pause and really listen to your spouse. By exploring all the possibilities instead of shooting everything down, you will get a fuller, clearer picture, and with that new perspective, you will have a more beautiful adventure than you can even imagine. Exploring makes a good adventure into a great adventure. Compromise can do the same for your marriage. Let's make today, the day of exploration.

CHAPTER 9

ENDLESS MILES, DETOURS, AND ROADBLOCKS (ENDURANCE)

Sometimes you have to embrace the suck

~ Andy McCall

T he skyline of St. Louis was a beautiful sight to behold. When Alex and I and the McCalls finally saw the buildings, we knew the long haul was over. We knew we were almost to our final destination. It had been a long 9 days, and an even longer last few hours, but we were almost there. We were about to eat the best barbeque in the United States.

I have talked a lot about our Grand Canyon trip in this book because it was a great trip and the Lord really used it to teach us a lot of lessons. The main goal was to skydive at the Grand Canyon, but we also had several smaller goals we wanted to accomplish as well. Alex and I wanted to share something with the McCalls that we had already experienced, the best barbeque in the United States. Alex and I had taken a random trip to St. Louis on our way home from Texas once, and a friend of ours told us about a restaurant called Pappy's that we should try while we were there. The food is phenomenal, so we decided, after we left the Grand Canyon, we would go up through Utah and Colorado, spend some time there, then shoot across Kansas, eat at Pappy's in St. Louis, and then start our descent into Alabama. This seemed like a great plan. Honestly, it was a great plan; however, there was one thing that none of us accounted for- the miles between us and the barbeque!

I'm sure you are thinking "miles" you have been driving for 9 days and you didn't account for the last few miles?!? Let me explain what I mean. The trip to the Grand Canyon was so very scenic. There were canyons, deserts, and mountains. There was so much to see on our way to the Grand Canyon, and then, after we left there we went into Utah and Colorado. Those two states are some of the most beautiful states I have ever seen. You are in the midst of the Rocky Mountains and it is breathtaking. Everywhere we looked there was something beautiful the Lord had created. We were constantly pointing and oohing and awing at something. We left the Rockies and had a straight shot from there to St. Louis through Kansas.

Here is where the problem came. Kansas is a part of the Great Plains region, although that area holds its own beauty, it's completely flat with very little to see scenically. Especially if you are doing a straight shot on the interstate. So, we left a place that was very aesthetically pleasing, for an area that was flat, and we were just passing through on our way to get barbeque. We had food on the brain and nothing to take our minds off of it. For 7 plus hours, we drove through Kansas thinking and talking about barbeque, eating every snack we had, and growing more bored by the minute. We had seen beautiful mountains and deserts. We had jumped out of a plane at 15 thousand feet at the Grand Canyon. We had hiked at 12 thousand feet elevation and had a snowball fight in June in Colorado. We had camped in the Rockies and we had the promise of the best barbeque in the United States ahead of us. However, we had to put in the miles if we were going to get to it. We had to endure the flat, seemingly endless miles to get where we wanted to go and to eat what we wanted to eat.

The miles from the Kansas state line to Pappy's Smokehouse, 671 miles to be exact, never seen to end, but we kept going! Did we complain, yes! Were there moments we questioned whether this barbeque was worth it, yes! Did we give up, no! Because we endured the miles, we got what we were going for, Pappy's! We received the promise we were searching for, barbeque!

The Promise Awaits

Just like we had the promise of barbeque ahead of us while we were traveling through Kansas, we all have the promise of a happy marriage if we choose to pursue it. We can be happily married to the same person regardless of whatever situations might arise. The difference between a couple that makes it to their promise and a couple that doesn't is one word- endurance. Endurance was one of the first words I wrote on my list when I started writing this book. I have been looking forward to writing this chapter since day one because this one thing can make or break a marriage. Whether or not you choose to endure, determines whether your marriage is going to last. Every marriage will run into endless miles, detours, and roadblocks as they navigate this journey of life. In fact, most of our days will just be us going through the endless routines of life. It's easy to look at the mundane and get tired or disappointed because everything always looks the same and the promise of change seems so far away. Then, there are the detours and roadblocks that occurred when the bad or unexpected things happen in our relationship. These times shouldn't be a shock for us because Jesus told us in John 16 that everyone will experience hard times at some point. I'm glad Jesus gave us this warning and the encouragement with it that even in those times He would be with us, but even with the warning those moments still come as a surprise and blindsided us at times. Endurance is the way we press through and stay on track to reach our destination during these times of trial. The couples that endure are the couples that make it where they are going.

Let's be honest though, no one wants to endure anything these days, just look at the divorce rate. Everyone wants the adventure, but without the miles. Everyone wants things to be scenic and beautiful all the time. Everyone wants the barbeque without Kansas. Don't get me wrong, that would be very nice; however, that's not how life works. Things will never be one hundred percent perfect all the time. Our marriages will not be one hundred percent perfect all the time. In our marriage adventure, there will be breathtakingly beautiful moments. Moments that are so perfect we can't even wrap our brains around them. These are the scenic moments we all love and want all the time. However, there will be mediocre moments when the miles of life just seem to drag on and on with no end in sight. We know what our promise is, but it seems so far away and it's very easy, in those moments, to start questioning whether the destination is worth the miles required. Then, even worse, we can have moments of unexpected detours and total roadblocks in our marriage where we totally get off course. These moments can be frustrating and even scary because we seem so lost and getting back on track seems impossible. We find ourselves sitting on the side of the road wondering how we got there and what we need to do to get back on course.

Unfortunately, a lot of marriages never get back on course. One or both people ditch the adventure altogether because they believe it isn't worth the effort. They buy into the lie that says if it isn't easy, then it isn't right. There are people out there bouncing from one spouse to another looking for the "perfect" spouse, when the "perfect" spouse doesn't exist. There are no perfect marriages and there are no perfect people. There are just imperfect people who are willing to fight for their marriages by choosing endurance over defeat. If you want your marriage to work and you want to arrive at your destination, you and your spouse will have to learn to enjoy the beautiful moments, but to endure the miles in between, and not give up when you come to a detour or a roadblock. In this final chapter, will we be talking about what endurance is, what endurance isn't, and how through endurance our marriages can grow regardless of the endless miles, detours, and roadblocks that life throws our way. I could think of no better way to end this book than by talking about endurance. The challenge here is to never give up on your spouse or your marriage. The adventure is there, your destination is possible, and the promise is attainable. We just have to make up our minds not to give up. We must learn to endure!

You Have A Need

For you have need of patient endurance [to bear up under difficult circumstances without compromising], so that when you have carried out the will of God, you may receive and enjoy to the full what is promised.
HEBREWS 10:36 AMPLIFIED VERSION

Let's start by learning what endurance means. Google tells us that endurance means *the fact or power of enduring an unpleasant or difficult process or situation without giving way.* Endurance simply means to not give up. To set a goal and to do everything it takes to accomplish that goal regardless of how the situation looks. It means you don't throw in the towel when things get hard but continue forward. I personally like how my friend Andy defines endurance. His definition of the word is, "Sometimes you have to embrace the suck." There are things that can be avoided in this life, and if that's the case, avoid them, but there are some things we just have to go through. Nobody likes the endless miles, but if you want to get to certain places you have to hunker down and keep pressing the gas pedal. You have to pass through in order to arrive. There are times in life the most important thing you can do it just hold on, continue forward, and not give up.

In Hebrews, it tells us we have a need for patient endurance if we're going to carry out the will of God in our lives. So, if that's the case, what is God's will when it comes to marriage? For that answer, let's look at what Jesus said in Matthew 19:1-9. The Pharisees have come to Jesus to try and trick him into saying something they can use against Him. They tried this tactic a lot with Jesus with various subjects, on this particular day, they bring up divorce. They are hoping they can get him to say something contradictory to scripture here because Moses had given certain stipulations where divorce was permitted. As always Jesus rises to the occasion and stops the Pharisees in their tracks. I encourage you to read the whole chapter, but we find His response to their questions in verses 5 and 6.

'For this reason, a man shall leave his father and mother and shall be joined inseparably to his wife, and the two shall become one flesh'? So, they are no longer two, but one flesh. Therefore, what God has joined together, let no one separate."
MATTHEW 19:5-6 AMPLIFIED VERSION

According to this verse, God's will for marriage is plain- stay married. I love the wording of the Amplified Bible when it says, "a man shall be joined 'inseparably' with his wife". That one word says it all, inseparably means to be united. This unity is meant to be permanent. If we are going to carry out that part of God's will, endurance is something we will have to implement in our lives and in our marriages. We must make up our minds we are not going to give up on our spouses. We must make up our minds we are not going to give up on our marriages. We must guard our hearts against the lies our society is screaming at us. The lie that says marriage is a joke and worthless. The lie that says your spouse is replaceable whenever things get messy or hard. Amid these lies, and whatever season of marriage you're in, we must hold tightly to the truth and maintain unity with our spouse. We must commit to the permanency of marriage. We must hold on tightly to the truth that marriage is God's idea and it's such a good idea. That marriage is valuable and precious. That marriage takes work, but it's worth the work. There are good days and bad days. There are days things fall into place so effortlessly and then there are days where everything is a struggle. In a world that is so loud with lies about marriage, here is some bold truth I would like to proclaim over you.

The person you married is the one God created for you! On the good days and the bad days, they're the one. We have got to get the "I made a mistake." or "They aren't right for me." mentality and chunk it! That kind of mentality will not help you to endure, it only enables the idea that divorce is ok. Our marriage is a beautiful adventure on the days that are scenic, but it's also a beautiful adventure on the days where the miles seem to never end. The way we take hold of that truth is by making the intentional decision to endure regardless of whatever the day brings. The adventure is worth the miles. We are a work in progress, so are our spouses and so are our marriages. God never gives up on us which tells me we should never give up on ourselves, our spouses, or our marriages. Divorce is not, nor will it ever be, God's will for your life, but I also believe to be miserable in your relationship is not God's will either. So, let's find the Biblical balance we need here. Since God's will is for us to stay married, let's find out how we can do that happily. Let's look deeper into how patient endurance can change our marriage into a beautiful adventure. Let's see how we can keep moving forward toward our promise with our spouse!

What Endurance Is and What It Isn't

We should never give up on our marriages, but I think sometimes we have a misunderstanding of certain things and I don't want that to happen here. I don't want you to go into this idea of patient endurance with a skewed understanding of what it means to endure something. Endurance is not passive and lazy. Endurance is not enabling situations that need to change. Endurance is not allowing things to continue in the same way with no hope of improvement. Endurance is definitely not staying in a dangerous or abusive situation. God hates divorce; however, He loves His children and there are certain situations where separation needs to happen for the safety of everyone involved. I'm not advocating for staying in a marriage that is physically abusive and dangerous. I believe abusive situations can be changed, and those marriages can be restored, BUT that can only happen if the abuse stops and BOTH people involved get the help and guidance needed.

When it comes to abuse it is never ok! NEVER! It's never deserved, and it should never be tolerated. If you are reading this and you are in an abusive relationship, please seek help. If you are in this kind of relationship, you can't fix it by yourself, so please don't try. Get the help that is needed. If your spouse wants to change, great, the Lord can bring restoration, but if they don't, do not stay in a dangerous situation. Don't think for a moment that's God's will for your life. Don't think for a moment endurance means taking the punch!

When I say to endure, I'm talking about the non-harmful experiences of life. Are there major problems that can arise where abuse is not present, yes! Are these problems hard, yes! Should we work through these instead of walking away, yes! We have people giving up on marriages that aren't abusive or dangerous, they're just in hard seasons. They're giving up because they would rather give up than do the work required. If there are areas in your marriage that need improvement or even a total change, then put in the work to do that. I am not saying "endure" a situation by just dealing with it and not addressing it. There are things that need to be dealt with head-on. I'm not saying to "endure" by lying and saying things are perfect when they aren't. Some situations need a change! What I am saying is, we should "endure" by making choices to strengthen our marriage instead of just walking away when things get messy. There is a difference in enduring something as you are passing through it and enduring something by never changing it.

Endurance is active. It's saying I am not going to quit, but I am going to do everything in my power to improve this. Endurance is saying this is not fun, but this is also not permanent. Endurance is hopeful and optimistic, but also truthful. Endurance is seeking help when it's needed and not covering up harmful situations. When we choose to "embrace the suck" we are acknowledging that things are not ok. We are not putting on rose-colored glass and pretending everything is perfect. Life and marriage can be hard, but by enduring we can be fully honest about our current situation, but at the same time be active in making decisions that will change our situation for the better. We can look at a bad situation in the face and say we will get through this together.

There is a Lesson to be Learned

And we know [with great confidence] that God [who is deeply concerned about us] causes all things to work together [as a plan] for good for those who love God, to those who are called according to His plan and purpose.

ROMANS 8:28 AMPLIFIED VERSION

The Lord is so detailed, and His desire is that we are constantly growing into the person that He wants us to be. He uses both good and bad situations to grow us. Most of the time when we encounter endless miles, detours, or roadblocks we only see the negative. We start the pity party prayers of "Why me, Lord?" and "Please take this away!". I have definitely prayed my fair share of these kinds of prayers. It's hard to see the positive of a bad situation while you're going through it. But, Romans 8:28 tells us God causes all things to work together for our good. It doesn't say all things are good, but that He will work it out for our good. What does that even mean? It means in every situation we can come out of it better than we went into it if we will let God do His full work. It means there is a lesson God has for us to learn that will grow us if we will take the time to learn it. It means maybe there is something in us that needs changing, and the Lord loves us enough to change it. I believe the Lord, like any good father, wants His children to be happy, but He also wants us to continually grow and mature and He will use any means necessary for that maturity to happen. He will sacrifice our happiness temporarily for growth to happen that will change us permanently for the better. So, as you're looking at your own marriage, what is the struggle that you're going through right now? What is the detour or roadblock you have come upon? What is an area of weakness you're experiencing? Now, instead of just looking at the problem and seeing it as negative, let's flip our perspective. Let's look and see if there is something the Lord is trying to teach us through this. Let's ask ourselves some questions.

- What Lessons Can "I" Learn from This?

There is always a lesson the Lord is trying to teach us. Some are easier to learn than others. But let's take a moment and prayerfully ask God what He is trying to teach us with whatever our current struggle is. Let's also take our eyes off our spouse for a moment while we ponder this question. When you thought about your situation and then thought about the lessons that can be learned, I'm sure you instantly thought of several lessons your spouse needs to learn, right? It's always easy to point to someone else and expose all the areas where they fall short, and all the lessons that they need to learn, especially if you live with them. But let's turn this question inward. Let God deal with your spouse for a moment and you focus on the part you play. No one is perfect and we're not called to be holy spirit junior to our spouses. The change may have to start with you. You may be the one that needs to change, period. There have been so many times during a detour or roadblock that I have prayed for God to change Alex. In every one of those situations, without fail, the Lord has told me to let Him worry about Alex, but while we were talking, He would be more than to glad to go over some areas in my life that could use some improvement. When my shortcomings are exposed, it never feels good at that moment, because I really don't like to come face to face with what I need to change. No one likes to see areas where they have fallen short; however, that's exactly what we need. We need to know these things about ourselves so we can continue to grow and mature. If we never see a need for change, no change will happen.

I challenge you to seek God and be open to the idea there are areas that need changing in you. It's never fun to be the one under the magnifying glass, but my goodness, it's necessary. Earnestly seek God, turn your focus inward, and explore what needs to change in you. According to Revelation 3:19, the Lord corrects the ones that He dearly loves. I am so glad this verse is in the Bible. Correction never feels like love when you are walking through it. This verse has helped me to remember that the correction is coming from a loving Father, not a harsh taskmaster. The Lord loves us too much to leave us where we are. Receive this as loving correction, not harsh discipline. At the end of the day, when you learn the lesson the Lord is trying to teach you, you and your marriage will be better for it.

- What Actions Can "I" take to Improve It?

Once you have done some self-examination, ask yourself what you can do to change your situation. I have heard it said that, the definition of insanity is doing the same things over and over; but expecting a different result. If that is the case, let's take the insanity out of our marriage. We can't continue to do the same old things and expect our marriage to get better. We can't continue to use the same words and the same actions and expect a different relationship with our spouses. So, with that in mind, once you have talked to God, make the changes that need to be made. When you see areas that need change ask the Lord to help you change them. The Lord will meet you in this and will walk with you through it. He doesn't ask us to fix ourselves all on our own, He's always there willing to help us. Also, ask the Lord to make you a fast and active learner. Ask Him to give you wisdom into what to do and then obedience and boldness to walk it out. If we will let the Lord do His full work in our lives, there are some situations we can get out of quicker. Mark Batterson is an author and the Lead Pastor of National Community Church in Washington, DC. One of the things he says all the time is, "pray like it depends on God, but work like it depends on you." This is a perfect thing to do as you are walking through a difficult or mundane time in your marriage. Talk to God often about whatever your situation is, but then do the work you need to do to change it for the better. God will do His part if we actively do our part.

- What Changes Can "We" Make as a Couple?

Once you have done a lot of talking with the Lord, sit down and talk to your spouse. This may be an awkward conversation since you will be talking about parts of your marriage that are not ok. But "embrace the suck" and have the conversation. Just be careful with your words here. Remember you are not holy spirit junior. It's all about the delivery. Come at it from a place of ownership of your part in the situation and from a desire of wanting the situation to improve. Come at it with tons of grace and love. Be open and honest with your spouse. If the Lord has shown you the areas in your life you need to change, share those with them and let them know you are working through them. Ask them to hold you accountable as you make these changes. Ask for forgiveness for any hurt you may have caused your spouse. Encourage them to get alone with the Lord as well. If this conversation goes well, then get a game plan. Talk about the areas where you both want to see change. Create action steps to make that change happen. Then walk those action steps out as a team. Cheer each other on and lift each other up when things start to improve. Show tons of grace and love when one or both of you slip and fall back into old habits. Continue to communicate with your spouse through all of this. This isn't a one and done conversation. Work as a team, ask the Lord to help, and you will see change as you patiently endure.

Detours and Roadblocks

So, maybe after reading all of that, you're thinking, "That's all well and good but what if my spouse is not on board to improve the situation? What if I have talked to them and that conversation did not go well? What if they have walked away from me? What now?" First off, if you find yourself in a situation where your spouse has given up on your relationship or doesn't seem to want to do anything to help fix what is wrong, I am so sorry. I'm sure that's an unbelievably hard spot to be in. Teamwork always works best when there are people that want to work as a team. However, my encouragement to you is to continue to endure. Sometimes teamwork starts as one person doing everything in their power and not giving up and that is what turns the team around. Two verses came to mind when I was thinking about roadblocks in our marriages.

Be on guard; stand firm in your faith [in God, respecting His precepts and keeping your doctrine sound]. Act like [mature] men and be courageous; be strong.
1 CORINTHIANS 16:13 AMPLIFIED VERSION

Therefore, put on the complete armor of God, so that you will be able to [successfully] resist and stand your ground in the evil day [of danger], and having done everything [that the crisis demands], to stand firm [in your place, fully prepared, immovable, victorious].

EPHESIANS 6:13 AMPLIFIED VERSION

When I read these verses I instantly think about soldiers in battle. As Christians, we have an enemy that is out to kill, steal, and destroy. He will do anything in his power to destroy us and our marriages. We are in a battle not only for our souls, but always for our relationships. We have got to fight against his attacks and sometimes it may feel as if you are the only one fighting for your relationship. Know this, you are not alone in this fight. Your spouse may not be fighting alongside you, but Jesus is. Jesus desires for your relationship to be whole and He will never stop fighting with and for you. So, whether or not your spouse continues to fight, don't give up! Stand your ground! At the end of the day, we cannot and will not have to answer for the decisions our spouses made, but we will be accountable for our decisions and actions. You can't control what your spouse does, but if you do everything in your power, at the end of the day, regardless of the outcome, you can hold your head high knowing you did everything in your power to stand.

One of two things will happen when you decided to do everything in your power to make your marriage work. One outcome is your relationship will be restored. I know of marriages that have been totally restored simply because one person in the relationship decided to not give up and because of that the other one did a complete turnaround. Restoration is possible. However, the opposite could happen, and your spouse could make the heartbreaking decision to walk away and not come back. In that case, press into God. We serve a God that is all-knowing, all-loving, and will never leave us or forsake us. In those moments, we must press in and not project that negativity on God or on ourselves. Yes, maybe your spouse did reject you, but you serve a God that accepts you right where you are! Maybe you had a spouse that did abandon you, but you serve a God that promises that He will never leave you or forget about you. Make the decision daily not to turn that negativity inward. Hold tightly to Psalm 136:1. *"Give thanks to the Lord, for He is good, for His steadfast love endures forever."* The love of your spouse may have failed you, but God's love never will.

Even here you are still enduring, just in a different way. You endure by moving forward knowing you are still a valued and loved child of God. Your value and worth do not go away if your spouse decides to walk away. Your relationship status doesn't determine your status with the Lord. So, in those moments when you seem to have come to a total roadblock, do your very best. Do everything you can do to make the marriage work, knowing you are accountable for your actions and your actions alone. When you have done everything to stand and you have done everything in your power to make things work, then regardless of the outcome, hold your head high knowing that you endured. You did everything possible! And you are still loved and accepted by God.

Protect Your Marriage

*I have fought the good and worthy and noble fight, I have fin-
ished the race, I have kept the faith*

2 TIMOTHY 4:7 AMPLIFIED VERSION

Marriage is a beautiful thing, but it's under attack. Every day, everywhere you look, you can find ways marriage is being portrayed negatively. Everywhere you look you can see the side effects of this negativity. Every day there are couples throwing in the towel and giving up on each other and on the idea that marriage can work. If we want our relationship to be different, we must protect it. If we're going to endure this life and arrive at our destination, we have got to do everything in our power to protect and nourish our most valuable relationship. Endurance is not passive. It's something we will have to choose to do every day in an active way. There will be days it will be crazy easy and there will be days it will be unbelievably hard, but every day it will be worth it. When I stand before the Lord, I want to look back at my marriage, grasp Alex's hand tightly, and say the same thing Paul did in 2 Timothy but with a few added words.

Lord, Alex and I fought the good fight. We went on this adventure together and we arrived together. It wasn't always easy, but my goodness was it beautiful!

Your adventure is ahead of you and you can make it to your promise! It's there, it's possible, and you have an awesome God that knows every mile you will encounter and is more than willing to help you with everything you will come upon. This adventure is long, and it will take work, but it's beautiful, and it's worth everything you will have to put into it! Endure the miles, find the lesson in the detours, and do everything in your power to get through the roadblocks you may experience, and you will get to your promised destination. Never, ever give up on yourself, your spouse, or your marriage! A happy marriage is possible! You can do this! You can have a beautiful adventure! Keep moving forward!

YOUR DESTINATION AWAITS

As I sit down to write out the conclusion of this book, I have just gotten home from a 9-day adventure with my love. Alex and I went to the west coast and had the chance to explore parts of Washington, Oregon, California, and Nevada. Each state, although so different from the next, had its own beautiful sights, sounds, smells, and experiences. The Lord met us there and showed us some amazing things and spoke to us in unique ways. We explored Seattle and learned as much as we could about the grunge movement that happened there in the '90s, went to the first Starbucks, and saw the majestic Mt. Rainier. We drove the US 101 down the breathtakingly gorgeous Oregon coast and saw sea lions and put our feet into the icy cold water of the Pacific Ocean. We went into California and walked amongst the giants in the Redwood forest, then drove across the snow-capped Sierra Nevada Mountains into the 107-degree heat of Death Valley. On this trip, we saw all kinds of different landscapes and experienced every kind of weather imaginable. We finished our trip by going into Las Vegas and renewing our vows before coming back home. Through this trip, I have learned several things that I have applied to my marriage.

One thing I learned is my place is with my God and with my Alex. If I have those two, I am where I am supposed to be. It doesn't matter where I live or where I go, when I have these two men in my life, I'm in the midst of an adventure and it is wild and beautiful. I don't have to strive to find my place or work to maintain it. It may not always look the way we want it too or feel the way we want it too, but as long as we choose not to give up and as long as the three of us partner with each other the outcome will always be a good one. My prayer is that you claim this for your marriage as well. Your God and your spouse, along with the determination to make the relationship work, are all you need to be successful in marriage. There is not a magic formula for marriage. It doesn't matter what kind of marital history your family has, your past mistakes, or what the enemy of your soul or the people around you say about you or your marriage. If you will commit to God and your spouse, you can have a beautiful adventure.

Another thing that I learned is there is beauty in everything. I mentioned earlier every state we went to on this recent trip was different, but each one held its own beauty. We saw rocky beaches, snow-capped mountains, sandy deserts, and majestic forests. Everywhere Alex and I looked, we saw something amazing. We made the comment several times about how different every place was, but how beautiful every place was as well. The same is true for our marriages. My marriage doesn't have to look like someone else's to be considered beautiful. Every marriage is different from the next, but that doesn't make one marriage right and the other wrong, in fact, it's those differences that make them unique and special. Your marriage doesn't have to look like anyone else's. In fact, it can be completely yours, completely different from others, completely different from mine, and completely beautiful. Your marriage will not always look the same either. Just like we experienced every climate change on this trip your marriage will experience different seasons also. Things may not always be sunny and warm, but don't be discouraged, because seasons come and go and bring with them something that's needed to grow. Don't determine the beauty of your marriage based on how your marriage compares to others or by whatever season you're currently in. We are all on our own adventure and different is not bad. There is beauty in everything.

One Decision

As we come to the end of this book, Alex and I pray, somewhere in these pages you have found something that has helped to strengthen your marriage. That you have committed to continue your adventure, make it beautiful, and hopefully someday help another couple on theirs as well. I didn't write this book because I have all the answers on marriage. I wrote it because the wisdom Alex and I received from the Lord, and the people He placed in our lives, helped us and we wanted to help others. Alex and I love being married and we want people to know how absolutely wonderful it can be. We dream of a day when divorce has been destroyed and healthy, happy marriages are everywhere you look. We dream of the day that married couples, partner with younger couples, and encourage and spur them on by telling them how good it's all going to be. We dream of the day marriage is looked at by all as a beautiful adventure. It's a lofty dream, but we serve a big God. He is able and we get to partner with Him to make this dream a reality.

It really all comes down to making one decision. If you are going to go on an adventure it starts with the one decision on where you are going. The same concept works with your marriage decision. One decision is all it takes to make your marriage great. One decision to put God first and invited Him into your marriage! One decision to forgive your spouse or yourself. One decision to put your spouse above yourself and pursue them passionately. One decision to be faithful and loyal. One decision to trust and have peace in your marriage. One decision to compromise when it's needed. One decision to endure and not give up. You are literally one decision away from turning your marriage completely around. You are one decision away from your own beautiful adventure. Make one decision and then continue to make it every day. When you take that one decision and make it a consistent thing in your marriage change will come, and we will be one step closer to that dream becoming a reality.

Show Us Wild and Beautiful Things

At the beginning of chapter 8, I shared the prayer I pray over all of our adventures. *"Abba, show us wild and beautiful things. Meet us there and speak to us in ways that only we will understand."* I always pray this right before we leave, and my sweet Daddy God always answers it in the most amazing ways. I have already shared with you some of the stories that still blow my mind of how God took the time to show up and speak to us through a change of scenery, but honestly there are so many others that I could share with you. I believe one reason He always answers this prayer is that one, we believe He will and two, we are looking for Him and expecting it. We have eyes and ears that are open and receptive to Him. We are actively looking and listening for Him. I want to close this book by praying this over your marriage. The wording will be a little different, but the request is the same. Pray this over your marriage with me and then expect the Lord to answer it. Look for Him in the everyday details of your life and your marriage and you will find Him. Pray to Him, then quietly listen, and believe He will answer you. He will show up and be a part of your life and your marriage if you will look and listen for Him. Of this I am certain.

"Abba,

We want the marriage that You created for us. Show us how wild and beautiful marriage can be. Speak to us in unique ways that will draw us closer together as we draw closer to You. Meet with us and give us the wisdom to make the daily decisions needed for a successful marriage. We need You, Lord! Come be a part of our lives and this sacred relationship! Lead us on the adventure that you have planned for us and let us see the beauty of it every day! Thank you for giving us this wonderful gift. Marriage was Your idea and it's such a good idea! We love you, Lord!

Amen"

Today is the day!

Your destination is attainable!

Enjoy the journey!

A beautiful adventure awaits!

Let's Go!

Acknowledgements

Alex Payne~ You are my greatest adventure! I wouldn't want to do this life with anyone but you! The Lord knew I would require a little extra help, so He gave me a pastor husband. You are just what I needed. You love me and believe in me, even in the moments that I didn't believe in myself. Your encouragement and the occasional push/drag in the right direction is the only reason this book became a reality. You are the man for this job, Alex Payne, and I will love you, for forever.

Penny and Andy McCall~ The Lord sure knew we need you guys! We were in a hard season when we met you two, but you took us in and spurred us on with your love and support. Thank you for believing in Alex and I. Thank you for mentoring us. Thank you for taking us along on your own adventure and giving us such wisdom and guidance. May we have many more adventures together!

Pastor Mike and Mrs. Sharon~ You gave us the tools at the start to make our adventure the best it could be. Thank you for forcing us to do premarital counseling and just being real with us up front. It seemed so insignificant at the time but the investment you made has paid off greatly for us. We can't thank you enough!

Kay, Tara M, Michelle, and Jana~ The Lord had put it on my heart to write a book, but I keep brushing it off. I wouldn't have taken the plunge had it not been for you guys speaking up and confirming the dream! Thank you for listening to the Lord and then being bold enough to share it with me!

Martin~ You rendered Alex and I speechless (which is not easy to do) with your generosity in making this dream a reality. You have been a blessing for our entire family. May the Lord bless you beyond what you can even think or imagine!

Kimberly Grammer~ You are so uniquely gifted by God! Thank you for your support and creativity with not only this book but also our ministry. Thank you for your honest critiques! They made this book better and of THAT I am sure!

To all my wild and crazy friends who believed~

In Mark 2:1-12 you find the story of the four crazy people that brought their paralyzed friend to Jesus so he could be healed. When they found they couldn't reach Jesus because of the crowd, they climb on the roof, opened the ceiling, and lowered their friend down to Jesus' feet. My summary of this story is this: sometimes you just need 4 crazy friends who refuse to give up. Friends who will carry you to Jesus, as often as necessary. I have been so abundantly blessed with more than 4 crazy friends. I wish I could list all the names, but you know who you are! You all are beyond creative and talented! You are wild in your faith, crazy in your passion, and you have laid me at the feet of Jesus in your prayers and lifted me up with your words more times than I could even recall or imagine. I love you all big! I could not have done this without your love, prayers, time, and talents! I know you all are world changers, because the Father has used you all to change my world.

Resources

~ **Jess Connolly**
  www.jessconnolly.com

~ **A Beautiful Adventure Marriage**
  www.abeautifuladventuremarriage.com

~ **Dr. Gary Chapman, "The 5 Love Languages"**
  https://www.5lovelanguages.com/

~ **Beth McCord**
  www.yourenneagramcoach.com

~ **Dave Ramsey, Financial Peace University**
  www.daveramsey.com

~ **Ryan and Selena Frederick, "Wife in Pursuit: 31 Daily Challenges" and "Husband in Pursuit: 31 Daily Challenges"**
  www.fiercemarriage.com

~ **Mark Gungor**
  www.markgungor.com

~ Mark Batterson

www.markbatterson.com

~ Paragon Skydiving

www.paragon-skydive.com

~ Pappy's Smokehouse

www.pappyssmokehouse.com

9 781400 330263